DE PROPRIETATIBUS LITTERARUM

*edenda curat*
C. H. VAN SCHOONEVELD
*Indiana University*

*Series Practica, 12*

# THE
MORALITY-PATTERNED
COMEDY OF THE
RENAISSANCE

*by*

SYLVIA D. FELDMAN

*Rutgers University*

1970
MOUTON
THE HAGUE · PARIS

© Copyright 1970 in The Netherlands.
Mouton & Co. N.V., Publishers, The Hague.

*No part of this book may be translated or reproduced in any form, by print, photoprint, microfilm, or any other means, without written permission from the publishers.*

Printed in Hungary

*For My Mother and Father*

# PREFACE

This study is concerned with the relationship between the morality play and Renaissance comedy. Another examination of the influence of the morality play upon English drama, at first, might seem to be superfluous; for the morality has received a good share of scholarly attention. Such attention has resulted because the morality play has an essential role in the development of English drama, especially that of the sixteenth and the seventeenth centuries. Allardyce Nicoll, for example, considers that with the morality, "...drama begins to move into the light of the modern age".[1] And A. P. Rossiter emphasizes the significance of the morality for a proper understanding of Renaissance plays: "...what might be called 'the Morality habit-of-mind' is a medieval heritage of the first importance to the understanding of Elizabethan drama".[2]

Scholars have found that the contributions of the morality play to the development of English drama are many. J. A. Symonds sees it as a transition between miracle plays and drama using individuals.[3] Bernhard ten Brink and Wilhelm Creizenach contend that the morality aided the development of invention, since playwrights were not bound to Biblical stories as they were in mystery plays.[4] Willard Farnham argues that the morality had 'tragic

---

[1] Allardyce Nicoll, *British Drama: An Historical Survey from the Beginning to the Present Time* (4th ed.; London, George G. Harrap and Co., Ltd., 1949), p. 41.

[2] A. P. Rossiter, *Early English Drama* (London, Hutchinson's University Library, 1950), p. 80.

[3] John Addington Symonds, *Shakespeare's Predecessors in the English Drama* (new ed.; London, Smith, Elder, and Co., 1900), p. 116.

[4] This is a view held generally by many early critics. See, for example, Bernhard ten Brink, *History of English Literature*, translated by William

potentiality' and, therefore, contributed to the development of Renaissance tragedy.[5] E. J. Burton believes that "...the morality encouraged the start of professionalism in the theatre...".[6] In 1962, David Bevington studied the influence of the dramatic companies performing morality plays upon the structure of later drama, especially that of Marlowe.[7]

The relationship between the morality play and comedy, particularly Renaissance comedy, has received some attention, although less than one might assume. In general, scholars have considered the contributions to be relatively few. Thomas Parrott and Robert Ball, for example, believe that the "old dramatic forms, Miracle, Moral, and Interlude" influenced Renaissance drama in three ways: through realism, that is "...the attempt to tell in dramatic form a story, sacred or profane, in such a way as to bring its truth home to the audience"; through the use of "...lively action on the stage. The Morals and Interludes of the sixteenth century tend more and more to discard expository and didactic speeches and to substitute entertaining dialogue and action"; and through the use of the comic characters of the Devil and the Vice.[8] Tucker Brooke argues that the morality play began the tradition of 'vulgar farce'.[9] As early as 1903, however, Charles Gayley suggested a very different effect:

> The heart of the 'moral' hero was a battleground; as in comedy, the interest was in the vicissitudes of the conflict and the certainty of peace. Though the purpose of the moral play was didactic and reformatory, its

---

Clarke Robinson (New York, Henry Holt and Co., 1893), p. 304, and Wilhelm Creizenach, "Chapter III, The Early Religious Drama, Miracle Plays and Moralities", *The Cambridge History of English Literature*, edited by A. W. Ward and A. R. Waller (New York, The Macmillan Company; Cambridge, The University Press, 1933), V, Part I, 60.

[5] 'Tragic potentiality' and the morality is an important aspect of his book. Willard Farnham, *The Medieval Heritage of Elizabethan Tragedy* (New York, Barnes & Noble, Inc., 1936, reprinted with corrections, 1956).

[6] Ernest James Burton, *The British Theatre: Its Repertory and Practice, 1100—1900* (London, Jenkins, 1960), p. 47.

[7] David M. Bevington, *From Mankind to Marlowe* (Cambridge, Harvard University Press, 1962).

[8] Thomas Marc Parrott and Robert Hamilton Ball, *A Short View of Elizabethan Drama* (New York, Charles Scribner's Sons, 1943), pp. 27-28.

[9] C. F. Tucker Brooke, *The Tudor Drama* (Boston, New York, Chicago: Houghton Mifflin Company, 1911), p. 48.

doctrine was optimistic and its end to encourage; and one of the distinctive contributions of the moral play to the English comedy was the movement suitable to these conditions, not the introduction of a continuous or connected plot.[10]

Unfortunately, Gayley did not develop the implications of this insight. Yet what he stated is, I believe, significant for Renaissance comedy. And the hypothesis upon which this work is based has led to exploring and expanding what Gayley implied.

I wish to thank Professors George Sensabaugh, Paul Kocher, and, in particular, Virgil K. Whitaker, of Stanford University. They read this work with careful concern when it was first prepared as a dissertation. In this revision I remain indebted to them for their judicious comments.

---

[10] Charles Mills Gayley, ed., "An Historical View of the Beginnings of English Comedy", *Representative English Comedies: From the Beginnings to Shakespeare* (New York, The Macmillan Company, 1903) I, lxiv.

# CONTENTS

Preface .................................................. 7

I. The Hypothesis ...................................... 13

II. The Morality Pattern, a Definition ................... 40

III. Evolution, as Reflected in Some Tudor Moral Interludes  65

IV. The Morality-Patterned Comedy .................... 91

Conclusion ............................................ 137

Appendix ............................................. 138

Bibliography .......................................... 151

Index ................................................. 160

I

THE HYPOTHESIS

This study is based upon the hypothesis that a category of Renaissance drama exists which has not yet been recognized. Its purpose is to isolate and describe the characteristics of that category: the morality-patterned comedy. It involves seventeen plays, the main plots of which have formal elements in common. The central core is composed of five plays: *How a Man May Chuse a Good Wife from a Bad* (c. 1601–1602), written, perhaps, by Thomas Heywood; *The Faire Maide of Bristow* (1603–1604); *The Dutch Curtezan* (1603–1604) by John Marston; Part I of *The Honest Whore* (1604) by Thomas Dekker and Thomas Middleton; and *Eastward Ho* (1605) by Ben Jonson, George Chapman, and John Marston. The remaining twelve plays use most of the formal elements but include some variation: *Misogonus* (c. 1560–1577), written, perhaps, by Laurence Johnson, Thomas Richards, or Anthony Rudd; *A Looking Glasse for London and England* (1587–1591) by Robert Greene and Thomas Lodge; *Histrio-mastix* (1589–1599), revised by John Marston; *All's Well That Ends Well* (c. 1601–c. 1604) by William Shakespeare; *The London Prodigal* (1603–1604); *The Wise-Woman of Hogsdon* (c. 1604?) by Thomas Heywood; Part II of *The Honest Whore* (1604–c. 1605) by Thomas Dekker; *The Miseries of Enforced Marriage* (1605–1606) by George Wilkins; *If This Be Not a Good Play, the Devil's In It* (1611–1612) by Thomas Dekker; *Match Me in London* (c. 1611–c. 1613) by Thomas Dekker; *The Staple of News* (1626) by Ben Jonson; and *The Lady of Pleasure* (1635) by James Shirley.[1] As this listing

[1] The dates and authors for all plays discussed in this work are taken from Alfred Harbage, *Annals of English Drama 975–1700*, revised by S. Schoenbaum (London, Methuen and Co., Ltd., 1964). Because of the difficulty of dating Renaissance and earlier plays precisely, I employed the limits, not the specific year assigned.

shows, the category consists of Elizabethan, Jacobean, and Carolinean works written by various popular playwrights. A description of its characteristics should contribute, therefore, to our general knowledge of Renaissance drama as well as to our better understanding of the individual plays.

A brief explanation at this point of what is meant by a morality-patterned comedy will be useful to the reader, although it anticipates what the remainder of the study will demonstrate. A morality-patterned comedy is a Renaissance work employing the didactic intention, character groupings, action, and structure of the morality play. It is not allegorical, however, because characters and plot are treated realistically. Two of these terms need to be defined. By 'action' is meant the essential conflict which a play dramatizes, by 'structure' the steps by which this action is developed. The differences between 'action' and 'structure' will be discussed in more detail in Chapter II.

An investigation of the formal elements of the oldest English morality plays occurs also in Chapter II. But a summary of this material will clarify the explanation given in the preceding paragraph. The didactic intention of the morality, usually stated at the beginning and end of the play, is to lead the members of the audience to eschew vice, repent their sins, and embrace virtue so that they may achieve spiritual salvation. The characters fall into three groups, each representing a moral position in a Christian universe. The central character is a mankind figure, who represents typical fallen Christian man, torn between his sensual and spiritual natures. Although his sensual nature leads him into a life of sin, he is capable of repentance and, consequently, potentially worthy of salvation. The Vices are those dramatic personae who tempt mankind to damnation while the Virtues are those who seek to bring about his regeneration. The action centers in the conflict between the Vices and the Virtues for the possession of mankind's soul. It always ends with the Vices defeated and with mankind repentant and absolved of sin through divine mercy. The structure of a fifteenth century morality consists of seven steps: the Vices are introduced; the mankind figure is introduced in a state of virtue; he is tempted and falls; his life in sin is shown; he is tempted to despair of mercy; he repents, that is, his faith in divine grace is restored, he is contrite, he confesses his sins, and he usually does penance; finally, he is forgiven. This structure may be varied slightly. If the play opens with the mankind figure in the midst of his life in sin, the first three steps are omitted. From this point on, however, the structural elements are the same. The problem of mankind's spiritual vision is central to the development of the action. Blinded by his sensual nature, mankind falls because he does not recognize the Vices for the evil forces they are. His regeneration begins with the correction of his spiritual vision: he recognizes that he has sinned and that his companions have threatened his spiritual well-being; then, usually with the help of a virtue character, he realizes that despite his sins, and because he has repented, he is worthy of divine forgiveness. These formal elements are the basis of a morality-patterned comedy.

As will be shown in Chapter IV, non-allegorical plays using these elements are comic because they accord with Renaissance theories of comedy. Their didactic intention fulfills a typical comic function: to demonstrate the need to avoid vice and to live virtuously. Their characters are those appropriate to comedy: that is, they are most often middle-class citizens, and the plot deals with their private affairs. Most important, the basic morality structure is in essence a comic structure, for it moves from turbulence to tranquility and it always ends happily.

If we assume that no art form is born full grown, that it is developed from and indebted to its predecessors, then we should not be surprised to discover that some Renaissance comedies have their roots in the morality play. The morality pattern was certainly durable. Alfred Harbage lists ninety-two 'morals', 'moral interludes', and 'moral masks' written between 1500 and 1652.[2] Willard Thorp states that the morality play dominated English drama until 1585 and that "... it was a truly national art form..."[3], one, according to Hardin Craig, that Shakespeare knew because moralities were "... still being written throughout his lifetime".[4]

---

[2] *Ibid*. The list presents some problems, for Harbage includes works which I do not consider to be moralities, cf., *The Peddlar's Prophecy*.

[3] Willard Thorp, *The Triumph of Realism in Elizabethan Drama, 1558–1612*, ("Princeton Studies in English", No. 2; Princeton, Princeton University Press, 1928), p. 20.

[4] Hardin Craig, *English Religious Drama of the Middle Ages* (Oxford, The Clarendon Press, 1955), p. 388. Dr. Craig's conclusion is supported by Thomas Heywood's *An Apology for Actors*, which includes the 'moral' as one of the accepted dramatic genres of his day. (Thomas Heywood, *An*

The number written and their continuing performance demonstrate that the form was extremely popular. It is, therefore, reasonable to postulate that morality elements, which offered the Renaissance playwright a successful pattern for comic organization, were used in non-allegorical plays. The evolution from morality play to morality-patterned comedy will be considered in Chapter III, an investigation of selected sixteenth century moral interludes. The rest of Chapter I, however, is devoted to investigating the hypothesis that such a category of Renaissance comedy exists.

For this purpose, *How a Man May Chuse a Good Wife From a Bad* (1601–1602), which is often attributed to Thomas Heywood, will be analyzed. This play is important in any study of Renaissance drama because it provides an example of an Elizabethan 'hit'. Its immense success is indicated by the seven printings it underwent during the seventeenth century: 1602, 1605, 1608, 1614, 1621, 1630, and 1634.[5] A popular work is always worthy of particular attention because it suggests the tastes of a wide audience and the ways playwrights catered to those tastes.

Furthermore, the play has elements in common with eight works written sometime between 1601 and 1605: *All's Well That Ends Well*, *The Dutch Curtezan*, *The London Prodigal*, *The Faire Maide of Bristow*, *The Wise-Woman of Hogsdon*, *The Honest Whore*, Parts I and II, and *Eastward Ho*. Except in *The Honest Whore*, Part I, and *Eastward Ho*, the central character is either a faithless husband or a faithless fiancé. He is a prodigal in all except *The Honest Whore*, Part I, *The Dutch Curtezan*, *All's Well*, and *The Faire Maide*. A courtesan is a major character in *How a Man May Chuse*, *The Dutch Curtezan*, *The Faire Maide*, and *The Honest Whore*. A faithful wife or a faithful fiancée, contrasted with the courtesan when she appears, is omitted only in *The Honest Whore*, Part I. Though the type varies, an intended crime is a frequent plot device. In all, the discovery of the hero's crime, his admission of guilt, repentance, and forgiveness occur. But for the possible exception of *All's Well*, *How a Man May Chuse* is the earliest of these works. It is possible, therefore, that as a result of its immense popularity, it influenced

---

*Apology for Actors*, edited by Richard H. Perkinson; New York, Scholars' Facsimiles and Reprints, 1941, F4).

[5] E. K. Chambers, *The Elizabethan Stage* (Oxford, The Clarendon Press, 1923), IV, 19.

those plays written and performed shortly after it which reveal similar formal elements.[6] The work is, consequently, of particular historical significance.

*How a Man May Chuse* deals with the spiritual education of Young Arthur, a middle-class Londoner who is a prodigal and a faithless husband, squandering his funds at the Exchange and ignoring his fair and virtuous wife. His motives for doing so are never explained. His disdain for his wife, for example, can only be justified by perverse willfulness; as he says,

> My reason is my mind, my ground my wil,
> I will not loue her: if you aske me why
> I cannot loue her, let that answere you.[7]

His present attitudes and actions, however, indicate that he has fallen from his previous state of virtue. Speaking of his son's marriage, Old Arthur informs the audience that:

> There was great hope, though they were matcht but yong
> Their vertues would haue made them simpathise,
> And liue together like two quiet Saints. (ll. 79-81)

Blinded by his will, Arthur proves himself incapable of judging his companions and his actions properly. His wife is hateful to his sight but Mary, a courtesan, bewitches him. In order to satisfy his lust, Arthur plans to murder his wife so that,

> From out her graue this Marigold should grow,
> Which in my nuptials I wold weare with pride. (ll. 1012-13)

---

[6] The plays may have influenced each other as well. Arthur Hobson Quinn, editor, *The Faire Maide of Bristow* ("Publications of the University of Pennsylvania Series in Philology and Literature", Vol. VIII, No. 1; Philadelphia, Ginn and Company, 1902) believes *How a Man* is the model for *A Faire Maide*, pp. 11-13. But C. R. Baskervill points out that it is probable that *How a Man* and *The Dutch Curtezan* are both sources ("Source and Analogues of 'How a Man May Choose a Good Wife From a Bad'", *Publications of the Modern Language Association of America*, XXIV, New Series XVII, 1909, p. 724).

[7] *How a Man May Chuse a Good Wife From a Bad*, edited by A. E. H. Swaen. "Materialien zur Kunde des alteren Englischen Dramas", Vol. XXXV. (Louvain, A Uystpryst, 1912), ll. 36-38. Other references to the play will be made in the body of the text.

At a dinner party purporting to celebrate a reconciliation with his wife, Arthur brings his wife a cup of poisoned wine. His plan fails only because he has actually given her a sleeping draught, one powerful enough, however, to convince him that he is free to wed the courtesan.

His wife is buried alive but is saved from death by Anselme, an unsuccessful wooer, who comes to her tomb at the moment of her awakening. He promises to hide her at his mother's home and to keep her recovery secret. In the meantime, Arthur marries again. Mary, he finds, is a bad wife, willful, unkind, extravagant, and immodest. He begins to long for what he has lost: "I had a wife would not haue vsde me so" (l. 2219) and begins to admit the folly of this second marriage, as his "God is just" (l. 2219) shows. But he does not yet fully understand Mary's nature or admit his own sinful state. In order to demonstrate his love for her and so to win her loyalty to him, he tells Mary of his supposed murder. She betrays him, and Arthur becomes a fugitive.

Refused help by his relatives, he is on the verge of despair and possible suicide:

> O whither shall I flie to saue my life,
> When murther and dispaire dogs at my heeles? (ll. 2341–42)

But he is saved from committing suicide by Mistress Arthur, whom he meets accidentally. Certain that she is dead, he does not recognize his first wife. He confesses his crimes to her, although, at first, he pretends that they are not his but rather those of a kinsman. His awareness of his sins and his sorrow for them are clear:

> He whom I term'd my friend, no friend of mine,
> Prouing both mine and his owne enemie,
> Poysoned his wife, o the time he did so,
> Ioyed at her death, inhumane slaue to do so,
> Exchang'd her loue for a base strumpets lust;
> Foule wretch, accursed villaine, to exchange so. (ll. 2405–10)

Mistress Arthur gives him hope of forgiveness:

> ...your rainie drops keepe;
> Repentance wipes away the drops of sin. (ll. 2428–29)

Once he has confessed, Arthur no longer tries to evade punishment. Recognizing that he was his "...own soul's foe" (l. 2444), he gives himself up. He confesses publicly to the supposed murder and begs forgiveness from all those he has wronged. Once he has undergone the humiliation of publicly admitting his crimes, Mistress Arthur appears to clear her husband of the murder charge. The trial serves, therefore, as Arthur's punishment for intended crimes. That he undergoes such punishment willingly is proof of regeneration. No longer blind to the dangers of sensual desire, the now virtuous Arthur is forgiven his trespasses and is restored to his proper position as the beloved husband of an exemplary wife.

This summary raises four questions which must be answered in order to discover the category of Renaissance drama to which *How a Man May Chuse* belongs. First of all, is the play tragic or comic? Second, how much of it is due to its novella source? Third, what changes in the source can be explained as the result of turning narrative into drama? Finally, what major elements remain to be accounted for? The first question establishes dramatic genre, the second and third eliminate those elements which are related to its source, and the fourth points up those remaining elements by which the play can be identified as belonging to a particular type of drama.

The play is clearly a comedy according to traditional Renaissance critical formulae.[8] The main characters are those traditionally considered appropriate ones for comedy, that is, they are all middle-class citizens, and *How a Man May Chuse* deals with their troubled but private affairs. What they do affects society only in the sense that "no man is an island", that any break in the social order weakens it. Arthur, of course, ignores his social responsibilities when he is prodigal and faithless and when he attempts to murder his wife. The work, moreover, begins in trouble and ends in peace as Arthur moves from a state of sinfulness to one of virtue. The episodes, no matter how threatening they may appear, contribute to this comic movement. Mary's betrayal, for example, brings about Arthur's realization of his sins but not his death; he is saved from possible suicide by a fortunate meeting with his first wife; and, most important, his crime, because it was intended but never achieved, can be paid for without affecting the happy ending typical of comedy.

---

[8] For a discussion of these formulae, see pp. 133-135.

The comic movement of *How a Man May Chuse* is to some extent due to its source, Novel V of Cinthio's *Hecatommithi*, probably drawn from the version which appeared as Novel 6, "Of Gonsales and his wife Agatha", in Barnaby Rich's *Farewell to Military Profession* of 1581.[9] The play follows that source closely: Gonsales, a Spanish merchant, attempts to poison Agatha, his virtuous wife, so that he will be able to marry a courtesan. His crime having been discovered, the merchant is sentenced to death. Unknown to him, however, Agatha has actually been given a sleeping potion, and at the last moment, Gonsales is saved from execution by her appearance.

While much of the plot's machinery depends upon this source, significant alterations have been made to turn novella into comedy written for an English audience. The setting has been moved from Seville to London, and the characters have been Anglicized so that the play mirrors contemporary London middle-class life.[10] Old Arthur and Old Lusam, the fathers of Young Arthur and his wife, have been added for expository, comic and structural purposes: they inform the audience of necessary background, such as the age of the couple, Arthur's previous state of virtue, his present prodigality, and his ill treatment of his wife; their discussions about their children are frequently humorous; and they further the plot development by bringing a legal suit against Arthur for mistreatment of his wife. Gonsales's friend, who woos his wife, substitutes the sleeping draught for the poison, and saves Agatha from burial alive, is replaced by three characters: Aminadab, a pedant and Mary's rejected suitor; Anselme, a nobleman who woos Mistress Arthur without success and visits her tomb at the very time she awakens; and Fuller, Anselme's comrade, who, fearing the pedant will carry out his threatened suicide, gives Aminadab a sleeping potion which he pretends is posion.

---

[9] Swaen believes, as I do, that Baskervill's conclusion that Rich's story is the source for the play is correct. See Swaen's introduction to *How a Man May Chuse*, pp. xiv–xvi and Baskervill's article, pp. 711–730. Thomas Mabry Cranfill, ed., *Rich's Farewell to Military Profession, 1581* (Austin, University of Texas Press, 1959) further supports Baskervill's findings; see pp. xxxix–xl.

[10] That comedy should mirror daily life was, of course, a common critical concept. See, for example, *An Apology for Actors* by Heywood, p. [F 1], which is, in turn, a summary of the essays of Evanthius and Donatus.

Major elements in *How a Man May Chuse* cannot be explained by the source or by the changes made to turn novella into drama. First of all, there is a general heightening of the conflict so that the choice between a good wife and a bad becomes as well a choice between Arthur's spiritual salvation and his spiritual damnation. The language in the play continually points up this spiritual conflict. One example should be sufficient here since most of the lines cited during the present discussion illustrate this same characteristic. At his trial, Arthur compares his first and second wives in terms of their moral positions in a Christian universe:

> I had a wife would not haue vsde me so,
> The wealth of Europe could not hire her tongue,
> To be offensiue to my patient eares,
> But in exchanging her, I did preferre
> A diuell before a Saint, night before day,
> Hell before heauen, and drosse before tried gold,
> Neuer was bargaine with such dammage sold. (ll. 2560-66)

In doing so, he suggests that by wedding Mary, he made a bargain with a devil and, consequently, threatened his spiritual well-being.

A statement of didactic intention reflecting the play's concern with the problem of spiritual salvation has been added. At the end of the play, Arthur sums up the moral significance of *How a Man May Chuse* for the audience:

> ...he that will chuse
> A good wife from a bad, come learn of me,
> That haue tried both, in wealth and miserie.
> . . . . . . . . . . . . . . . . .
> On this hand vertue, and on this hand sin;
> This who would striue to lose, or this to win?
> Here liues perpetual joy, here burning woe;
> Now, husbands, chuse on which hand you will goe.
> Seeke vertuous wiues, all husbands will be blest,
> Faire wiues are good, but vertuous wiues are best.
>         (ll. 2720-22; 2735-40)

The play's purpose, then, is to demonstrate the need for man to eschew vice, repent his sins, and embrace virtue if he is to achieve both earthly happiness and spiritual salvation.

The play's concern with the problem of man's spiritual well-being is evident in the development of the three central characters:

Mary, Mistress Arthur, and Young Arthur. Mary's profession as a courtesan immediately places her on the side of evil. Her evil nature is further established by her companions, Mistress Splay, a bawd, and Brabo, a swaggerer, and by the notorious reputation she has earned. Furthermore, she proves herself bent not only upon destroying Arthur's earthly happiness but upon bringing about his spiritual damnation as well. As she tells him,

> ...if I knew
> What in this world would most torment thy soule,
> That I would doo: would all my euill vsage
> Could make thee straight dispaire, and hang thy selfe. (ll. 221-24)

Mistress Arthur is contrasted with Mary in every way. She is, first of all, an exemplary wife, whose chastity, wisdom, and Christian virtue have earned her universal admiration. And clearly she is on the side of the angels. Young Lusam, for example, who knows Arthur and his wife, asks the husband:

> What is your wife a woman or a Saint?
> A wife, or some bright Angell come from heauen? (ll. 269-70)

Mistress Arthur tells Anselme that despite her husband's ill treatment, she will always attempt to protect him: even

> ...after death my vnsubstantiall soule,
> Like a good Angell shall attend on him,
> And keepe him from all harme. (ll. 2159-61)

She seeks, of course, Arthur's physical and spiritual welfare. Her appearance at his trial saves him from death. By listening to his confession and then giving him hope of forgiveness, she contributes to his regeneration and, consequently, to his spiritual salvation. In terms of a Christian view of man, Arthur is a typical human being. Although corrupted by original sin, and tempted by evil, he is also capable of good. His sensual nature may control his reason and blind him to his own spiritual condition and that of his companions; but he is, nevertheless, potentially worthy of salvation because he can and does turn from vice and embrace virtue.

On one level, then, we can say that the action of the play centers in the conflict between the forces of evil and good for the possession of Arthur's soul. Mary tempts Arthur to spiritual damnation while his first wife offers him the means of spiritual salvation. At the end, of course, the forces of evil are defeated.

This action is developed in four steps. The play opens with Arthur fallen from a state of virtue and in the midst of a life of sin, illustrated by his prodigality, his faithlessness to his wife and his lust for a courtesan. His sensual desires overrule his reason. As a result, he is unaware that he pursues evil and he is incapable of judging correctly the worth of his wife or of Mary. The second step consists of the temptation to despair. After Mary's betrayal, Arthur finally realizes the evil he has committed and he fears he is unworthy of forgiveness. The third step consists of his repentance. Contrite for his sins, Arthur confesses them to his first wife and, with her help, renews his faith that he can be forgiven them. His trial, which through the public airing of his follies serves to punish Arthur for his intended crimes, can be interpreted as a form of penance, since Arthur is made to pay and pay well for what he has done. Finally, the play ends with the regenerate Arthur forgiven his his sins and restored to his proper position as the virtuous husband of a virtuous wife.

None of the elements reflecting the play's very real concern with the problem of spiritual salvation are found in the source, and they cannot be explained by the changes necessary to turn novella into drama. They are, nevertheless, the basis of the play's dramatic unity and those elements which give it its distinctive nature. Can these elements be found within any of the traditional comic categories or within that of tragi-comedy? If not, the validity of the hypothesis upon which this study is based can be accepted, since *How a Man May Chuse*, and any other works which reveal the same elements, could then be placed in a new category, one which is based upon those qualities which distinguish it from other types of Renaissance plays. The establishment of such a category does not, of course, assume that Renaissance playwrights, while they may have consciously borrowed morality elements, were consciously working within a particular subtype of drama. For as we know, playwrights often were not and are not concerned about distinctions between genres. This category, therefore, should be considered simply a means by which we can more conveniently learn about and organize the elements which make up Renaissance drama.

The best way of ascertaining whether or not *How a Man May Chuse* belongs to any traditional category is to compare it with plays that do. For this purpose, it will be compared with five Elizabethan plays, four comedies and one tragi-comedy. The comedies represent obvious examples of specific types: Shakespeare's *As You Like It* is a romantic comedy; Chapman's *All Fooles* is an example of Latin situation comedy written by an English dramatist; *Supposes* is Italian comedy, drawn from Ariosto and "Englished" by Gascoigne; and Jonson's *Volpone* is a superb example of satire. Beaumont and Fletcher's *A King and No King* is included as a representative tragi-comedy. While the term 'tragi-comedy' is so broad" that it often has little descriptive value for modern scholars, in the works of Beaumont and Fletcher it refers to a particular type of Renaissance drama. Since *How a Man May Chuse* has a serious action with tragic potential and a happy ending, it will be useful to compare it with *A King and No King* in order to consider whether it may, after all, be considered a tragi-comedy. The choice of plays is arbitrary, although well-known works representing traditional categories have been selected. The only concern of the following discussions is to point out those elements which set *How a Man May Chuse* apart from the other plays.

Shakespeare's *As You Like* (1598–1600), despite some comical satire[12], is essentially a pastoral romance.[13] The play revolves around the complications of courtship and moves toward the ultimate and appropriate union of lovers. From the beginning of the play, Orlando and Rosalind are clearly well matched. Both are remarkable in their virtue. Rosalind, for example, is so beloved that the Duke decides to banish her because,

> ...her smoothness,
> Her very silence and her patience,
> Speak to the people, and they pity her.[14]

[11] See pp. 33–35 for a short definition of tragicomedy.

[12] Oscar J. Campbell *(Shakespeare's Satire*, London, Oxford University Press, 1943) believes that by means of satire, "The play thus ridicules the belief that life close to nature is best" (p. 48). He feels Jacques and Touchstone have satiric functions (pp. 48–64).

[13] The best discussion of the romance I found was in E. C. Pettet, *Shakespeare and the Romance Tradition* (London, Staples Press, 1949).

[14] William Shakespeare, *As You Like It*, in *The Complete Works of Shakespeare*, edited by George Lyman Kitteredge (Boston, Ginn and Company, 1936), I, iii, 79–81. Other references to the play will be made in the body of the text.

Orlando's excellencies are established by Oliver, who like so many villains, is capable of perceiving the good he wishes to destroy:

> ...he's gentle; never school'd and yet learned; full of noble device; of all sorts enchantingly beloved, and indeed so much in the heart of the world, and especially of my own people, who best know him, that I am altogether misprised. (I, i, 172-77)

Their noble rank, their virtues, and even their problems (for both are forced to flee injustice) make Orlando and Rosaling appropriate lovers. And most of the comedy results from complications which delay but do not seriously threaten the happy outcome of their love.

The ending of *As You Like It* illustrates the 'basic harmony' which Nevill Coghill considers to be part of Shakespeare's comic vision;[15] for here, as in most Shakespearean comedies, "...lovers are united, faults are pardoned, enmities are reconciled".[16] At the conclusion, not only the lovers' problems but all problems are resolved, including the tyranny and injustice with which the play opened. Oliver repents his treatment of Orlando and promises to restore him to his proper place. Frederick returns the usurped dukedom to its rightful ruler and enters a monastery. Evil is not punished, because it no longer exists but, like a dream, melts into thin air.

The forest of Arden, however much Anglicized, is, therefore, an enchanted world.[17] Misunderstandings and confusion exist, but, as far as we know from the play, evil does not. Significantly, both Frederick and Oliver enter the forest intent upon killing their brothers, but once in the forest they shed their evil natures. Frederick comes only to

> ...the skirts of this wild wood...
> Where, meeting with an old religious man,
> After some question with him, was converted
> Both from his interprise and from the world. (V, iv, 165-68)

---

[15] Nevill Coghill, "The Basis of Shakespearian Comedy", *Essays and Studies, 1950* (New Series; London, John Murray, 1950) III, 13.

[16] *Ibid.*

[17] This 'enchanted world' is what Northorp Frye considers 'the green world' of comedy. See *Anatomy of Criticism* (Princeton, Princeton University Press, 1957), pp. 182-86.

Oliver lives in the forest where he is reconciled with Orlando and married to Celia. Like him, all who live in Arden are rewarded because all there show themselves to be worthy.

Moral judgments about man's relationship to man are frequent. The maltreatment of a younger brother, for example, is acknowledged to be unnatural by Orlando and Celia. The dangers of a tyrannous ruler are suggested by Le Beau when he warns Orlando to leave the dukedom. And the evils of courtly life are dealt with superbly by Duke Senior when he compares the woods to the envious court. But such judgments are only part of the play's richness, not its controlling purpose, and they are always subordinated to the comic adventures of the lovers.

*How a Man May Chuse* is quite different. As the title and Arthur's concluding speech demonstrate, it is meant to be an exemplum from which the audience may learn how to achieve earthly happiness and spiritual salvation. At the beginning of the play, Arthur is not an appropriate husband for his virtuous wife because he is immersed in a sinful life and, consequently, blind to her worth. The plot deals with Arthur's spiritual education, one result of which is that he becomes a proper husband. Unlike Orlando and Rosalind, Arthur and his wife are ill-matched until the play's conclusion.

*How a Man May Chuse*, furthermore, is set in middle-class, Elizabethan London, where good and evil co-exist. Mary and Mistress Arthur, for example, are neighbors. A foolish judge hears the complaints against Arthur for his ill treatment of his wife, while Young Lusam comments wisely upon the judge's stupidity. Although good (represented by Arthur's regeneration and his reconciliation with his wife) triumphs over evil, evil continues to exist. Mary does not succeed in bringing about Arthur's physical and spiritual death, but neither does she repent her wickedness nor is she punished for her crimes. She remains free to live as she has been living and to threaten the well-being of others. Young Arthur, then, lives in a world where both good and evil are realities, but where man must choose which he will pursue.

Chapman's *All Fooles* (1599–1604), a Latin situation comedy based upon *Heautontimorumenos* and *Adelphi* by Terence, combines two plots, uniting them through Rynaldo, the primary manipulator of the action, who believes his

>   ...fortune is to winne renowne by Gulling,
>   Gostanzo, Darioto, and Cornelio:
>   All which suppose in all their different kindes,
>   Their witts entyre, and in themselues no piece.[18]

He manipulates, however, only to improve the fortunes of others. Fortunio, his older brother, loves Bellanora but because of Gostanzo, her father, is unable to court and marry her. Valerio, Rynaldo's friend and Gostanzo's son, has secretly wedded the beautiful and virtuous Gratiana, who has no dowry. Rynaldo manages the intrigue so that Fortunio and Bellanora are eventually married and so that Valerio and Gratiana obtain Gostanzo's blessing. He manipulates further to force the jealous husband Cornelio to realize the folly of jealousy by pretending to give him just cause.

Until the last act, the plot depends upon the intrigues Rynaldo invents to deceive Gostanzo and Cornelio. Gratiana is introduced to Gostanzo as Fortunio's wife. Gostanzo permits her to stay at his home until Fortunio can receive the blessing of Mark Antonio, his father. After a short time, however, he begins to suspect that his son has fallen in love with Gratiana and suggests that she and Fortunio leave. The lovers then confess to Mark Antonio the true state of their affairs. But Gostanzo convinces him that the account is untrue. Soon afterwards, Valerio tells his father the truth, that he is Gratiana's husband. Believing the lies, Gostanzo welcomes the girl as his daughter-in-law. When he later discovers he has been gulled, Gostanzo has no choice but to accept the marriage of Valerio and the penniless Gratiana, as well as that of Fortunio and Bellanora, who have, in the meantime, wed secretly. With the help of Valerio, Rynaldo manages the intrigue so that Cornelio believes his wife to have been Darioto's mistress, and the jealous husband decides to divorce her.

The resolution of many plays in which the plot depends upon a manipulator occurs because the manipulator has himself been gulled or because his plans are upset accidentally. In *All Fooles*, the former occurs: Cornelio deceives Rynaldo by telling him that

---

[18] George Chapman, *All Fooles*, in *The Comedies and Tragedies of George Chapman, Now First Collected with Illustrative Notes, and a Memoir of the Author in Three Volumes*, [edited by Richard Herne Shepherd,] Vol. I (London, John Pearson, 1873), 172. Other references to the play will be made in the body of the text.

Valerio is held for debt and that both must meet him at the Halfe Moone Taverne. He then arranges for Gostanzo and Mark Antonio to go there as well. The marriages are discovered, Rynaldo's intrigues are revealed, and he discovers that he too can be gulled. Finally, the sons and their fathers convince Cornelio to give up his intended divorce and to realize how foolish he has been; as Gostanzo states, "Hornes cannot be kept off with jealousie" (p. 185).

Rynaldo's intrigues on behalf of the lovers are necessitated by Gostanzo. He is a strict and foolish parent, who is more concerned about the wealth his children can bring him through advantageous marriages than he is about their happiness. Bellanora is a prisoner in her father's house, where, as she says,

> ...I as in a prison
> Consume my lost dayes, and the tedious nights,
> My Father guarding me for one I hate. (p. 127)

Valerio has been educated inappropriately, as Rynaldo's description of that education demonstrates:

> I haue knowne
> Your ioyes were all imployde in husbandry,
> Your study was how many loades of hay
> A meadow of so many acres yeelded;
> How many Oxen such a close would fat. (p. 118)

In order to assume his proper station as a gentleman, Valerio must rebel against his father:

> I hope I know
> I am a Gentleman, though his couetous humour
> And education hath transform'd me Bayly,
> And made me ouerseer of his pastures,
> Ile be my selfe, in spight of husbandry. (p. 118)

It is not until the last act that Gostanzo discovers his son, whom he thought a country bumpkin, to be, in fact, a gallant.

Gostanzo's folly is emphasized by contrasting him with Mark Antonio and his own children. Mark Antonio shows himself to be a better father, loving, trusting, and lenient, one who has earned the love and respect of his sons. His children show themselves to be wiser than Gostanzo because they recognize that virtue is worth more than wealth and that marriage with love is preferable to marriage for property.

Moral judgments are frequent in *All Fooles*. The last line of the play, for example, sums up the moral of the Cornelio sub-plot: "Hornes cannot be kept off by jealousie" (p. 185). Satirical comments about the faithlessness of women occur in dialogues between the Page and Cornelius and in Act V when Gostanzo and Valerio convince the jealous husband to give up the divorce action. The scene in which Gostanzo tries to teach Valerio that, "Friendship is but a Terme" (p. 134) satirizes avarice. In general, thenn *'All Fooles* abounds in comments ridiculing the vices of the time, but its intention is clearly not didactic or moralizing.

Gascoigne's *Supposes* (1566),[19] a close translation of Ariosto's *I Suppositi*, has much in common with Latin comedy.[20] The plot is one of intrigue necessitated by the avariciousness of Damon, Polynesta's father. Having fallen in love with Polynesta, Erastrato changes places with his servant Dulipo so that he can woo more easily. At the beginning of the play, Damon has decided to wed his daughter to the highest bidder. Erastrato and Cleander, an elderly lawyer, are her suitors. To win Polynesta, Erastrato has promised that he will match the dowry Cleander has offered and that his father will appear to make the pledge good. He and Dulipo intend to present a false Philogano, Erastrato's father, in order to fulfill the promise.

Erastrato and Dulipo, therefore, initiate the intrigue. But once it has begun, accident, rather than manipulation, complicates it. Philogano arrives unexpectedly to discover that another masquerades as himself. Damon learns of the affair between Polynesta and Erastrato. Believing Erastrato to be a servant, he puts the lover into prison. The resolution is achieved by accident and by explanation of the disguises. After he is told why Dulipo and Erastrato have exchanged places, Philogano forgives the servant

[19] George Gascoigne, *Supposes*, in *The Complete Works of George Gascoigne*, edited by John W. Cunliffe (Cambridge, The University Press, 1907), I, 187–243.

[20] Ariosto's play was drawn from Plautus' *Captivi* and Terence's *Eunachus*. See R. Warwick Bond's discussion of the relation of the play to its source and the influence of Latin comedy in his *Early Plays from the Italian* (Oxford, The Clarendon Press, 1911), pp. l–lxcii.

and fulfills the pledge his son has made to Damon. Dulipo is discovered to be Cleander's son, lost at sea eighteen years before. Since he has an heir, Cleander withdraws his suit for Polynesta. All ends well: the lovers are betrothed, and the sons are reunited with their fathers.

In addition to the use of accident as the major complicating device, *Supposes* differs from *All Fooles* in other ways. The discovery of a lost child (a frequent device in Latin comedy) does not occur in Chapman's work. And the crafty servant is used in *Supposes* rather than the crafty brother. Unity of time and place are kept as they are not in *All Fooles*, where the plot covers several days and the setting changes from a street, to the house of Gostanzo and Mark Antonio, and finally to a tavern. The plot of *Supposes* takes place within a few hours, and all the scenes are set in Ferrara, before the houses of Damon and Erastrato. While *All Fooles* contains a great deal of moral comment about contemporary vices, *Supposes* contains almost none, and, indeed, might well be considered almost amoral.

*How a Man May Chuse* differs in two significant ways from *All Fooles* and *Supposes*. First, it does not deal with the conflict between the foolish parent and the wise child which is essential to these plays. Old Lusam and Old Arthur may be humorous, but their condemnation of Young Arthur is just. Although stupid men exist in *How a Man May Chuse* (for example, the pedant and the judge), Arthur's follies are the play's only concerns. Second, and more important, the plot does not depend upon manipulation but, rather, upon the spiritual condition of the central figures. Mary and Mistress Arthur behave as they do because the one is corrupt and the other virtuous. Arthur commits crimes only because he is blind to the nature of evil; once he perceives it, he rejects vice and embraces virtue. The mistaken conclusion, used as a means of plot complication and resolution, occurs only when the sleeping potion is mistaken for poison by the desperate Aminadab and by Arthur, who takes it from him purportedly in order to prevent his intended suicide. Accident as a plot device is used twice: when Anselme visits the tomb at the moment of Mistress Arthur's awakening and when Arthur meets her while he is fleeing from justice. The first is necessary for the happy ending and the second is necessary for Arthur's spiritual regeneration.

As in Latin comedy, the plot of Jonson's *Volpone* (1605–1606) is manipulated, here by Mosca, a parasite, and by Volpone, his master. Accident, however, is used once as a complicating device: when Bonario happens to be in Volpone's house at the very moment the Fox attempts to rape Celia.

Jonson's Venice is a world degraded by avarice. Volpone worships money and through the hoax of seeking an heir feeds upon the avariciousness of others. Mosca manipulates the intrigue in order to outwit Volpone and obtain his wealth. Voltore, Corvino, and Corbaccio bribe the supposedly dying Volpone with gifts because each hopes to prey upon his remains. Indeed, it is precisely because they are so intent upon becoming his heir that the Fox's intrigues succeed at all. Blinded by avarice, they assume that they are the ones who gull.

The baseness of the three is unquestionable. Although they pretend to be virtuous, their hypocrisy is obvious. Corbaccio tries to poison Volpone, though he says the potion is "...but to make him sleep".[21] Corvino attempts to convince his wife that an affair with Volpone would not be an adulterous act. And Voltore, a lawyer, perjures himself to clear Volpone of the charge of attempted rape. Significantly, all three are old men. While the young may be expected to act foolishly, because they are 'unseasoned', their elders are expected to act wisely. Their spiritual corruption, therefore, is increased by the fact that they, who are approaching death and who should be the worthiest members of society, are instead the most depraved.

In a society where such men hold power, the community is endangered. As the first trial shows, good can be defeated by evil. Celia and Bonario are found to be guilty since they have no adequate defense against age and reputation. Truth cannot shine forth when those who should recognize it are blinded by the powerful but corrupt. The fools, Lord and Lady Politic, are controlled by the evil-doers and used to destroy virtue. The last trial indicates the extent to which avarice can destroy man's judgment. The Fourth Advocate prefers to believe Mosca innocent simply because, as Volpone's heir, the parasite would be "A fit match for my daughter" (V, xii, 51).

---

[21] Ben Jonson, *Volpone, or the Fox*, in *Ben Jonson*, edited by C. H. Herford and Percy Simpson, V (Oxford, The Clarendon Press, 1937), I, iv, 17. Other references to the play will be made in the body of the text.

The resolution of the plot occurs as the result of intrigue carried too far. Volpone gives out the report that he is dead and that Mosca has been made his heir. Having realized that he has been gulled and pretending to speak in order to clear his conscience, Voltore confesses that the evidence he gave in the first trial was perjured. To save himself, Volpone must admit that the report of his death is false. When Mosca refuses to confirm this fact, Volpone realizes that he, too, has been gulled, and he decides to take revenge upon Mosca by making their manipulations public. The evil-doers are unmasked, therefore, only when they betray each other.

Once unmasked, they are punished by society. Those who commit evil receive justice, but not mercy, for they are unworthy. As the First Advocate tells Celia, one should not plead for them; in doing so, "You hurt your innocence, suing for the guilty" (V, xii, 106). None of the evil-doers repents or shows any indication of change. Since they are incapable of regeneration, they must not only be punished but withdrawn from society as well. Mosca is sent to the galleys, Volpone to prison, Corbaccio to a monastery, and Corvino to be beaten publicly and shamed. Reparation is made to the innocent: Celia returns to her father with her dowry trebled, and Bonario inherits before his father's death. Good triumphs because evil destroys itself, winning its just rewards.

*Volpone* certainly is a satire meant to ridicule the vice of avarice, and its didactic intention is explicit. In the Prologue, Jonson states that his purpose, as in all his works, is "To mix profit with pleasure" (Prol., 8). At the end of the play, the First Advocate draws the moral for the audience:

> Let all, that see these vices thus rewarded,
> Take heart, and loue to study 'hem. Mischiefes feed
> Like beasts, till they be fat, and then they bleed. (V, xii, 149-51)

Moral instruction, therefore, is important in *Volpone* as it is in *How a Man May Chuse*.

For the most part, however, the two plays differ greatly. Much of this difference depends upon varying attitudes toward human nature. In *Volpone*, man is basically evil, while in *How a Man May Chuse*, he is basically good. In the latter, the virtuous characters outnumber the evil ones, and Mary is the only evil figure of any significance. She is, furthermore, the only hypocrite in the play, for she pretends to love Arthur in order to obtain his wealth.

Arthur, on the other hand, is blind but no hypocrite. He acts as he does only because he believes he loves the courtesan. Corvino, Corbaccio, and Voltore are perfectly aware of the evil nature of the acts they commit, but they continue on their course, justifying their actions by means of hypocrisy.

Unlike the evil-doers in *Volpone*, Arthur is capable of regeneration. He may not always act wisely, but, as the discussion of his prior life, the adoration of his wife, and his repentance demonstrate, he inclines toward virtue. And his life in sin is a lapse rather than an indication of spiritual limitations as it is for the avaricious men in Jonson's play.

The above discussion suggests that *How a Man May Chuse* differs from these traditional types of Renaissance comedy because of its world, characters, structure, action, and didactic intention. To recapitulate, it takes place in contemporary Elizabethan England, a world where good and evil coexist and where man must choose which he will follow. Its main characters, Young Arthur, Mistress Arthur, and Mary, are developed in terms of their moral positions in a Christian universe. Its structure depends upon the spiritual regeneration of Young Arthur. And its action deals with the struggle between the forces of good and the forces of evil for control of his earthly behaviour and spiritual well-being. Finally, the play is meant to be an exemplum from which the audience learns that, in order to attain earthly happiness and spiritual salvation, man must avoid vice and embrace virtue.

Because of these differences, one would not, I believe, place *How a Man May Chuse* in the same category with, for example, *As You Like It*, but one would never hesitate to call it comedy. One might well ask, however, whether *How a Man May Chuse* is true comedy at all — whether it is not, after all, tragi-comedy.[22] *How a Man May Chuse* certainly has a serious action, one which from a Christian view holds the potential for tragedy. And as in tragi-comedy the catastrophe — that is, the death and damnation of Arthur — is averted, and the play ends happily. Yet neither

---

[22] *How a Man May Chuse* as well as several other plays which I consider to be mortality-patterned comedies are considered 'tragical comedies' by Marvin T. Herrick in his *Tragicomedy* ("Illinois Studies in Language and Literature", Vol. 39; Urbana, Illinois Press, 1955), pp. 224–260. He argues that these are works which come close to tragi-comedy. Obviously, as my study indicates, I differ markedly in my convictions about such works.

the seriousness of the action nor the averted catastrophe are adequate justifications for considering the play to be tragi-comedy.

A serious action which has the potential for a tragic outcome belongs to comedy as well as to tragi-comedy. *As You Like It*, for example, contains problems which have tragic potential: brother hates brother, a dukedom has been usurped, the rightful ruler exiled, and lovers have met only to be separated. The lovers, of course, meet again almost immediately; but the other problems, which affect them, exist until the end of the play. Although there is no catastrophe of tragic proportions, the possibility exists that one might occur. Until Oliver asks Orlando's forgiveness and until Frederick is converted by the monk, the threat that one or both may enter the forest, kill his brother, and bring disaster is always present. For the most part, however, these problems are evaded, while the plot deals with the intricacies of courtship. The potential for a tragic outcome exists as well in *How a Man May Chuse*. The play deals with the problem of Arthur's physical preservation and spiritual salvation, developed through his attempted murder and climaxed by his trial. But that it should end unhappily is even less probable than that *As You Like It* should do so. The audience knows that Arthur has not poisoned his wife, and because of her devotion to him, they can assume he will not die for her supposed death.

The problem of classifying Renaissance drama is complicated by the fact that the term 'tragi-comedy' had several meanings in Renaissance drama. In Richard Edward's *Damon and Pythias* (1565?), for example, the term 'tragical comedy' indicates a mingling of tragic and comic characters, an averted catastrophe, and a happy ending.[23] Since the wicked sons are punished and the virtuous ones rewarded, Gascoigne considers *Glasse of Government* (1575) to be a tragi-comedy. *The English Traveller* by Thomas Heywood (c. 1607–1609), on the other hand, is so described because the main plot is domestic tragedy and the sub-plot is comedy.

Although 'tragi-comedy' is an extremely loose term, it does attain some precision when applied to the works of Beaumont and Fletcher. In their plays, it describes a particular form of drama which includes the following distinguishing elements: an exotic and romantic setting, an exotic and romantic plot, and

[23] See Herrick's discussion, pp. 224–227.

characters of tragic stature, noble in birth and feeling.[24] Little, if any, didactic intention is evident. Stress is laid upon 'the lively touches of passion' exhibited and upon the involutions of the plot. The play develops as though a tragic conclusion were inevitable; suddenly, by means of plot manipulation, the tragedy is averted and the play ends happily.

In order to demonstrate that *How a Man May Chuse* cannot be considered a tragi-comedy, it would be helpful to compare it with *A King and No King* (1611), a play which both Frank Ristine and Eugene Waith, have accepted as a fully developed tragi-comedy.[25]

*A King and No King* takes place in Armenia and Iberia. The use of this foreign setting allows the audience's "...imagination to wander at will, unhampered by the restrictions of reality".[26] Arbaces, the hero, is the King of Iberia; Panthea, his love and supposed sister, is a princess; Tigranes, his conquered enemy, is the King of Armenia. The central figures have, of course, nobility of character as well as noble rank. Arbaces, for example, is shown to be an extraordinary man. At the beginning of the play we learn that by overcoming Tigranes in single combat, he won the war with Armenia. Victorious, he would not think,

> The man I held worthy to combate me
> Shall be us'd serviley...[27]

---

[24] These elements combine those found in the discussion of Madeleine Doran (*Endeavors of Art*, Madison, The University of Wisconsin Press, 1963, pp. 190-215) and the discussions of two Beaumont and Fletcher scholars, Frank Humphrey Ristine (*English Tragicomedy, Its Origin and History*, New York, The Columbia University Press, 1910) and Eugene M. Waith (*The Pattern of Tragicomedy in Beaumont and Fletcher*, New Haven, Yale University Press, 1952). M. T. Herrick explains why I have chosen a Beaumont and Fletcher play, "...English tragicomedy arose gradually and from a variety of sources. Beaumont and Fletcher came at the climax of this gradual development; they could not have produced their particular tragicomedies without the lessons taught by the earlier writers of tragedies, comedies, histories, pastorals, and tragical comedies. While THEY MAY HAVE PERFECTED THE TYPE and established it as the most popular dramatic form in England during the first half of the seventeenth century, they did not introduce it". (p. 261, emphasis mine).

[25] Ristine, p. 28 and Waith, p. 36.

[26] Ristine, p. 111.

[27] Francis Beaumont and John Fletcher, *A King and No King*, in *The Works of Francis Beaumont and John Fletcher*, edited by Arnold Glover

With the generosity worthy of a king, he offers the defeated Tigranes the hand of his sister, Panthea. His faults, however, are as great as his virtues. Arbaces' pride is extreme, and his passions are, at times, so uncontrollable that, as his loyal servant tells him, they "...eclipse your virtues" (I, i, p. 158).

Arbaces' inability to control his passions initiates the plot. After he sees Panthea, whom he had not seen for nine years, he falls in love with her. Though he struggles against this incestuous passion, it is so great that he finally decides he must succumb to it:

> It is resolved, I bare it whilst I could, I
> can no more, I must begin with murther of my
> friends, and so go on to that incestuous
> ravishing, and end my life and sins with a
> forbidden blow, upon myself. (V, p. 222)

Torn by what would appear to be an irreconcilable conflict, Arbaces seems certain to bring destruction to his kingdom and himself.

The catastrophe, however, is averted. Just as he is on the verge of killing Gobrias, seducing Panthea, and committing suicide, Arbaces discovers that his love is not incestuous after all. For he is actually Gobrias' son, adopted prior to Panthea's conception by the Queen who feared her husband would die without an heir. His passion, then, is lawful and desirable since it will unite a noble ruler with the rightful heir of Iberia. The resolution of the plot occurs at the very moment that a tragic ending seems inevitable and depends not upon character development but upon plot contrivance. Arbaces is told facts about himself which, if disclosed earlier, would have concluded the play after Act II.

To a large extent, suspense and interest are achieved by controlling the audience's knowledge. At the beginning of the play, the audience knows only as much about the intrigues in the court of Iberia as Arbaces does himself. It knows that the king is noble but passionate, that his sister is extraordinarily beautiful, and that his 'unnatural' mother conspires against her son's life. Except for information about the love of Tigranes for Spaconia, its knowledge is limited to facts available to Arbaces, and so it is forced to share his viewpoint.

---

(Cambridge, The University Press, 1905), I, i, p. 152. Other references to the play will be made in the body of the text.

The dramatic intensity of the love scenes depends upon this manipulation of the audience's viewpoint. To cite one example, the scene between Arbaces and Panthea in which he tells her of his torment, avows his love, and hears her confess a growing passion for him would not be terrifying or touching if the audience knew that, in a few days, this passion would end in wedded bliss. The audience is tantalized by the potentiality for manifold horrors: patricide, incest, and suicide, to name only three. But it is finally satisfied by a resolution which evades all of these nicely and which brings about the wished-for conclusion. With Arbaces and Panthea, it shares the passion but none of the consequences which such a passion should bring.

'Lively touches of passion'[28] and involutions of the plot are the most striking elements of the play. But it fails to satisfy the modern reader, if not a Jacobean audience, because it presents no interpretation of life. As Waith says,

> One of the most important [conclusions] is that *A King and No King*, as Eliot once said perversely of Shakespeare's drama, has no meaning. It says nothing about incest, pride, jealousy or wrath, but it presents an arrangement of dramatic moments in which these passions are displayed.[29]

Whatever the limitations of *How a Man May Chuse*, it does comment upon man's responsibility to himself and to his society, albeit the comment is typically Christian.

Whereas much of the intensity of *A King and No King* results from controlling the audience's knowledge of essential facts, in *How a Man May Chuse* no such control is used. Instead, the audience has greater knowledge than the hero. It knows before he attempts to poison his wife that Arthur will give her a sleeping potion and that Mistress Arthur will live. Suspense, therefore, is not achieved by manipulation. Rather, it is achieved by the moral problem which the hero faces and resolves.

In both plays, the catastrophe is avoided. In *A King and No King*, this is done by eradicating the causes for Arbaces' conflict, that is, by making his love for Panthea lawful and desirable. In *How a Man May Chuse*, the catastrophe is avoided because Arthur is ready to live a virtuous life. Proof of his regeneration is found

---

[28] Waith, p. 39.
[29] *Ibid.*, p. 41.

in his realization that by pursuing Mary he has sinned and in his heartfelt repentance. Once he has turned from a life of sin, Arthur is forgiven and restored to his appropriate place in a Christian society.

While *How a Man May Chuse* differs significantly from the plays discussed above, it does have elements in common with them, elements which point out that Renaissance drama is ultimately the result of various influences. The novella source and Anselme's passion for Mistress Arthur are reminiscent of romantic comedy. The conception of Old Lusam, a foolish but well-meaning father, may have been influenced by Latin comedy, and Brabo, the swaggerer, surely has his roots in the *miles gloriosus*. Aminadab, the foolish pedant, may come from Italian comedy.[30] The setting and the social position of the characters in *How a Man May Chuse* are in the satirical-realistic tradition. And, as in satirical comedy, there is some ridicule of the vices of the time. Finally, like the plot of tragi-comedy, that of *How a Man May Chuse* contains the potential for tragedy, albeit domestic tragedy.

But whatever similarities *How a Man May Chuse* has with the five plays discussed, we could not put it into any of the categories to which the latter belong. The differences are simply too great.

The play differs from other types of comedy in three ways. First, it is separated by a didactic intention which they do not have. The purpose of *How a Man May Chuse* is to teach the members of the audience that the best means of attaining spiritual salvation and earthly happiness is by eschewing vice, repenting one's sins, and embracing virtue. Second, its central figures are developed in terms of this specific didactic intention, and they, consequently, represent moral positions in a Christian universe. Mistress Arthur is both a virtuous wife and a moral force which attempts to draw man from evil and toward good. Mary is the courtesan who tempts man to ignore his familial and social responsibilities and a destructive moral force that leads him to his spiritual damnation. Young Arthur is both an erring husband and a typical human being, tempted by evil but capable of perceiving its nature and then turning from it. Third, the play's action and structure separate it from other works. On one level, the action deals with the struggle

---

[30] See Bond's discussion regarding the influence of Italian comedy on English comedy, pp. xxix–xxx.

between those who wish to lead him toward behaviour which is socially approved. On another level, however, the action deals with the struggle between the forces of evil and the forces of good for possession of a Christian's soul. The structure develops the action concerning man's spiritual well-being in a particular sequence. It begins with Arthur in the midst of a life in sin, after a fall from virtue. His fall has made him blind to the spiritual worth of those around him. Once he begins to realize his sins, he is tempted to despair of forgiveness for them and tempted, therefore, to commit suicide. He repents instead — that is, he is contrite, he confesses his sins, he has hope of forgiveness, and he does penance. Finally, he is forgiven and restored to his appropriate position in a Christian society.[31]

These elements not only separate *How a Man May Chuse* from most other Renaissance comedies, but they suggest, as well, its dramatic origins and the category to which it belongs. The play is based upon traditional Christian dogma and is concerned, on one level, with the problem of man's spiritual salvation. The morality play has the same basis and the same concern. An investigation of the oldest English morality plays needs to be undertaken, therefore, in order to ascertain whether or not in these allegorical works may be discovered those elements which give *How a Man May Chuse* its distinctive nature.

---

[31] While I am generalizing the main characters of this play into types, I do not mean to imply that other characters in other plays cannot be generalized into types as well. In this study, however, I am concerned only with these particular types as they appear in this particular kind of play.

II

THE MORALITY PATTERN, A DEFINITION

Of the five plays considered to be the oldest English moralities, the earliest, *Pride of Life* (late fourteenth century), is a fragment and therefore useless for the purposes of analyzing the basic morality elements. The others, *The Castell of Perseverance* (c. 1405–1425), *Wisdom* (c. 1460), *Mankind* (c. 1465–c. 1470) and *Everyman* (c. 1495–1500),[1] however, should be adequate. These four plays

[1] In choosing these plays as the oldest extant moralities (or, as they may be referred to, 'the medieval moralities'), I am relying upon the work of previous scholars, particularly, C. F. Tucker Brooke *(The Tudor Drama*, Boston, Houghton Mifflin Company, 1911, pp. 47–68), Hardin Craig *(English Religious Drama of the Middle Ages*, Oxford, The Clarendon Press, 1955, p. 378), and Arnold Williams *(The Drama of Medieval England*, Michigan State University Press, 1961, pp. 142–162). E. K. Chambers considers these works to be five of the six moralities "...which can with any plausibility be assigned to the fifteenth century..." *(The Mediaeval Stage*, London, Oxford University Press, 1903, II, 155). He includes *Mundus et Infans*, however, as the other morality definitely to be so assigned although the work was first published purportly as a 'new interlude' by Wynkyn de Worde in 1522 (p. 155 and p. 439). He excludes Henry Medwall's *Nature*, which according to Pearl Hogrefe was "...doubtless written before 1500" (Pearl Hogrefe, *The Sir Thomas More Circle*, Urbana, The University of Illinois Press, 1959, p. 257) and "...probably published by William Rastell about 1530 to 1534..." *(Ibid.)* since he considers it a moral interlude. I have deferred discussion of both *Mundus et Infans* and *Nature* until Chapter III, a study of selected Tudor moral interludes, for two reasons: first, they are not among those plays traditionally grouped together as the oldest (or medieval) moralities; and second, according to the printed texts both are considered 'interludes' rather than 'moral plays'. (See Chambers, *Mediaeval Stage*, II, 439 and 443.) To use Chambers's definition, they were plays "...given in the banqueting-halls of the great". *(Ibid.,* p. 183.)

Also omitted from this chapter, and from the study, as well, are the miracle plays which contain morality elements, such as the Coventry *Massacre of the Innocents*, the Coventry *Salutation and Conception* and the

show that, excluding allegory (which is, of course, one distinguishing feature of a morality play), the primary morality elements are a single didactic intention, a single action composed of a single sequential structure, and particular character types, through which the action is developed and the didactic intention realized. Much of the following discussion includes material which scholars have already dealt with in some detail. But it is necessary to review this material because such scholarship is often contradictory or confusing.

The first point which must be made about the morality play is so obvious that one might, perhaps, forget its importance. An English morality play has a particular frame of reference, which determines its didactic intention, action, structure, and characters. Like all moralities, it is a play prepared for a Christian audience and based upon orthodox Christian dogma. Whatever conclusions are drawn about the morality play are done so within this context.

The problem which immediately arises in any discussion of the morality is the significance of allegory. While allegory is unquestionably a significant feature of the morality, it has, I believe, too often received more than its due; that is, too often it has been considered the single most important feature of the morality play. Twentieth century scholarship continues to reflect this attitude. Four examples should suffice, however, to indicate the great emphasis scholars have sometimes placed upon this particular feature. In his 1914 study of the English morality, Roy Mackenzie described it as drama which is "...allegorical in structure."[2] And in his 1914 study of English drama, Felix Schelling reached the conclusion that "...allegory is the distinguishing mark of the moral plays".[3] This emphasis has not changed in the last fifty years. In his excellent 1961 *Guide to English Literature* of the Middle Ages, David M. Zesmer, for example, defines the morality play for the student as "...a dramatized allegory, best exemplified in

---

Digby *Mary Magdalene*. I have done so because of the necessity of establishing limits to this study and because I feel that the four plays included here are adequate for the purposes of establishing the morality features.

[2] Roy W. Mackenzie, *The English Moralities from the Point of View of Allegory* (Boston and London, Ginn and Company, 1914), p. 9.

[3] Felix E. Schelling, *English Drama* (London, J. M. Dent & Sons, Ltd., 1914), p. 24.

Everyman".[4] And in his 1962 study of the relationship between the morality play and the structure of Renaissance drama, David Bevington echoes what was said half a century before; he states that the morality "...was characterized primarily by the use of allegory to convey a moral lesson about religious or civil conduct".[5]

Yet after the morality has been defined largely on the basis of allegory, we know relatively little about it. As Hardin Craig has said: "It is true that a morality play is a dramatized allegory and that no drama is a morality play unless it has this characteristic feature, but even this statement leaves the subject vague".[6] We must conclude, therefore, that the difference between the morality and other types of drama depends not only upon the use of allegory but also upon the combination of those formal elements which are the source of the morality's organization; for "The morality play is a special kind of play in which mankind, symbolically or allegorically presented, works out his only possible salvation."[7] The remainder of this chapter is devoted to discovering those formal elements which make the morality a 'special kind of play.'

After allegory, the most noticeable feature of the morality is its particular didactic intention, which, as we shall see, controls structure. The four moralities are unquestionably meant to be exempla. The second Vexillator of *The Castell of Perseverance*, for example, tells the audience the play has a didactic function:

Þe case of our comynge, ȝou to declare,
euery man in hym self, for sothe he it may fynde.[8]

The Doctor of *Everyman* ends the play by advising the members of the audience to reflect upon what they have just seen:

[4] David M. Zesmer, *Guide to English Literature from Beowulf through Chaucer and Medieval Drama*, "College Outline Series" (New York, Barnes & Noble, Inc., 1961), p. 269.
[5] David M. Bevington, *From Mankind to Marlowe* (Cambridge, Harvard University Press, 1962), p. 9.
[6] Hardin Craig, *English Religious Drama of the Middle Ages* (Oxford, The Clarendon Press, 1955), p. 341.
[7] Hardin Craig, "Morality Plays and Elizabethan Drama", *The Shakespeare Quarterly*, I (April, 1950), 68.
[8] *The Castell of Perseverance*, in *The Macro Plays*, edited by F. J. Furnivall and Alfred W. Pollard ("Early English Text Society", Extra Series, XCI; London, Kegan Paul, Trench, Trubner & Co., Ltd., 1904), ll. 14–15. Other references to the play will be made in the body of the text.

This morall men may haue in mynde.
Ye herers, take it of worth, olde and yonge.[9]

The didactic function of these moralities is so important that in all four plays a statement of didactic intention frames the action. *Wisdom* begins with a dialogue between Wisdom and Anima, in which the former instructs the Soul concerning its proper relation to God and ends with a warning to the audience to avoid sin. In *Castell*, the Prologue explains the play's action and its purpose; at the conclusion of the play, God reminds the members of the audience to think of Judgment Day and warns them to repent and to live virtuously. *Mankind* begins and ends with a sermon on the need for good works and virtuous living, and on sinful man's potential for salvation through divine mercy. The Messenger and the Doctor in *Everyman* point out to the audience that man's earthly life is transitory and that, consequently, man must think constantly of his spiritual salvation.

The didactic intention of these plays is exactly the same: to lead the members of the audience to eschew vice, repent their sins, and embrace virtue so that they may achieve the salvation of their souls. The last lines of *Castell* reflect this purpose:

> þus endyth oure gamys!
> To saue ȝou fro synnynge,
> Evyr at þe begynnynge
> Thynke on ȝoure last endynge! (ll. 3646-50)

Anima in *Wisdom* is just as explicit:

> Nowe ye mut euery soule renewe
> In grace, & vycys to eschew,
> Ande so to ende with perfeccion,
> That þe doctryne of Wysdom we may sew.[10]

In *Mankind*, Mercy advises the members of the audience to:

---

[9] *Everyman*, edited by A. C. Cawley (Manchester, Manchester University Press, 1961), ll. 902-03. Other references to the play will be made in the body of the text.

[10] *A Morality of Wisdom, Who is Christ*, in *The Macro Plays*, ll. 1164-67. Other references to the play will be made in the body of the text.

Serche 30ur condicyons with dew examinnacion !
thynke & remembyr, þe world ys but a wanite,
as yt ys prowyd daly by d[i]uerse transmutacyon.[11]

Finally, the Doctor in *Everyman* warns men that if one's

...rekenynge be not clere whan he doth come,
God wyll saye, 'Ite, maledicti, in ignem eternum.' (ll. 914-15)

This didactic intention is one means of distinguishing the morality play from other forms of drama. For while many plays are didactic and often explicitly so, only the morality play has the specific task of teaching man that he must always think of and strive for his spiritual salvation.

The didactic function of the morality leads to an action common to all four plays. By 'action' is meant the essential conflict which a play dramatizes. The steps by which this action is realized and their sequential relationship to each other is termed the play's 'structure'. 'Plot', on the other hand, consists of the unique handling of a story, through which the action is made concrete. *How a Man May Chuse* will demonstrate. The action of this comedy deals with the conflict between the forces of good (Mistress Arthur) and the forces of evil (Mary) for the possession of the body and soul of a typical Christian (Arthur). The structure develops this action in four steps: Arthur's life in sin, his temptation to despair, his repentance, and his forgiveness. The plot, however, deals with Arthur's treatment of his first wife, his lust for Mary, his attempted murder, and his trial. Through the plot, the action is particularized and the didactic purpose achieved. In the early moralities, 'plot' and 'action' are almost interchangable terms. There are, of course, some differences in the plot of each play. These differences, however, are less important than they are in a work like *How a Man May Chuse* and will be clear to the reader during the following discussions.

Although the action of the morality has received a good deal of scholarly attention, that one action is common to the moralities has not always been accepted. In his introduction to the Early

---

[11] *Mankind*, in *The Macro Plays*, ll. 901-03. Other references to the play will be made in the body of the text.

English Text Society edition of *Magnyfycence*, for example, Robert Lee Ramsey sees "three, or at the most four distinct plots", or what in this study are defined as actions: The Conflict of Vices and Virtues, that is, the struggle between the forces of good and evil in a Christian universe, the Debate of the Heavenly Graces, the Coming of Death, and the Debate of Soul and Body, of which "...no exemplar remains".[12] E. K. Chambers finds three: The Conflict of Vice and Virtue, which is the most important, the Reconciliation of the Heavenly Virtues, and the Dance of Death.[13] Roy Mackenzie sees two only: the Conflict between Vices and Virtues and the Summons of Death.[14] Some scholars, however, have argued that a single action exists in all moralities. Creizenach, for instance, states that, "The theme [action] running through all these plays is the contention between the personified good and bad powers of the soul for the possession of man...".[15] While he supports the judgment of Creizenach, Bernard Spivack is much more vague: "...the plot [action] of the morality play presents through visible forms and actions the invisible history of the human soul according to the Christian formulation".[16]

The extant moralities display a unity which, I believe, Ramsey, Mackenzie, and Chambers have not acknowledged. The Conflict of Vices and Virtues occurs in all four plays. In *Castell* it is the temptations of the World, the Flesh, and the Devil which draw Mankind from a life of virtue. The Virtues, Shrift, Penance, and the Seven Moral Virtues, lead him to repentance and to the Castle of Perseverance. Throughout the play, the Vices struggle with the Virtues for possession of Mankind's soul in order to bring about

---

[12] Of these four, Ramsey concludes that the Conflict of Vices and Virtues became 'the typical English plot', and that the Coming of Death occurs 'in combination' in *Pride of Life* and *Castle* but is the plot of *Everyman*. See: Robert Lee Ramsey (ed.), *Magnyfycence, a Moral Play by John Skelton* ("Early English Text Society", Extra Series, XCVIII; London, Kegan Paul, Trench, Trubner and Co., 1908), pp. cxlviii–cxlix.

[13] E. K. Chambers, *The Mediaeval Stage*, II, 153.

[14] Mackenzie, pp. 22–23.

[15] Wilhelm Creizenach, "Chapter III, The Early Religious Drama, Miracle Plays and Moralities", *The Cambridge History of English Literature*, edited by A. W. Ward (New York, The Macmillan Company; Cambridge, The University Press, 1933), V, Part I, 57.

[16] Bernard Spivack, *Shakespeare and the Allegory of Evil* (New York, Columbia University Press, 1958), p. 103.

his spiritual damnation. In *Wisdom*, Lucifer corrupts Mind, Will, and Understanding because he wishes to defile man's soul. Wisdom (Christ) helps them overcome the Devil and leads them to the path of virtue. In *Mankind*, the hero is tempted by Titivillus and his comrades to forsake the godly life; ultimately, however, with the aid of Mercy he repents and returns to a state of virtue. This conflict exists in *Everyman* as well. Before the moment of Everyman's life with which the play is concerned, the Vices have vanquished the Virtues and brought about Everyman's downfall. The play deals with the second part of the conflict between the Vices and the Virtues, in which the Vices are defeated by the Virtues because they turn Everyman from the forces of evil and potential spiritual damnation toward repentance and spiritual salvation.

The conflict between the Vices and the Virtues is, then, the one action common to the four moralities. This conflict, moreover, has only one object: the possession of mankind's soul. And it has, as well, only one outcome: while the Vices succeed for a time, the Virtues are the ultimate and permanent victors, for mankind always repents and, consequently, always saves his soul. The other actions mentioned by Ramsey, Mackenzie, and Chambers are related to this conflict. They are either a variation on this action, a complication resulting from it, or a motivation for its resolution.

The Debate of Body and Soul, which Ramsey considers an action for which no exemplar exists,[17] occurs briefly in *Castell* but is simply a variation of the conflict between the Vices and the Virtues. It cannot be separated from this conflict, for sin is always associated with sensual excess. According to *Wisdom*, sensuality is served by the five wits, and

> Wan þey be not rewlyde ordynately;
> The sensualyte þan, withowte lesynge,
> Is made þe ymage of synne, then of hys foly. (ll. 137-40)

This conflict, of course, is inherent in the composition of man; for just as the Vices struggle to control mankind, so does man's body strive to govern his soul. Mankind illustrates:

> My name ys 'Mankynde'; I haue my composycyon
> Of a body & of a soull, of condycyon contrarye:

[17] Ramsey, p. cxlviii.

> Be-twyx þe tweyn, ys a grett dyvisyon.
> He þat xulde be s[u]biecte, now he hath þe victory.
> Thys ys to me a lamentable story,
> To se my flesch, of my soull to haue gouernance (ll. 189-94)

In *Castell* the temptations that the Vices offer Mankind are those satisfying his sensual desires. Mankind's falls and repentances indicate, therefore, not only the struggle between the Vices and the Virtues but the continuing conflict between his sensual and spiritual natures as well. After his death, Mankind's Soul berates his dead Body because the Soul must now pay for the Body's pleasures:

> ...þou dedyst brew a byttyr bale,
> to þi lustys whanne gannyst loute;
> Þi sely sowle schal ben a-kale;
> I beye þi dedys with rewly rowte (ll. 3013-16)

"The Debate of the Heavenly Graces" forms only one section of one play, *The Castell of Perseverance*. Because Mankind has succumbed to the temptations of the World, the Flesh, and the Devil, Truth and Righteousness argue that he deserves to be damned; but Mercy and Peace contend that since he repented his sins, Mankind is worthy of divine grace. The "Debate", then, is simply a complication resulting from the conflict of the Vices and the Virtues for the soul of mankind. And its outcome demonstrates that unworthy but repentant man may, because God is merciful, achieve salvation despite his sins.

The Coming of Death occurs in the last section of *Castell* and in *Everyman*. The second repentance of Mankind in *Castle* is motivated by the coming of death, and this repentance concludes the conflict between the Vices and the Virtues for his soul. Because he repents the Vices are defeated and Mankind receives grace. Similarly, *Everyman* is motivated by the summons, which brings about the moment of awareness that is responsible for the hero's regeneration and, consequently, his spiritual salvation. As Lawrence Ryan has said, Everyman's "...excessive love of passing things has placed him in danger of hell-fire".[18] His spiritual regeneration depends

---

[18] Lawrence V. Ryan, "Doctrine and Dramatic Structure in *Everyman*", *Speculum* (October, 1957), 725.

upon his recognition that he has placed his love in unworthy and transitory objects, and it is through the Summons of Death that this is achieved.

In *Everyman*, therefore, one aspect of the conflict of the Vices and the Virtues is presented. At the beginning of the play, Everyman serves the World, the Flesh, and the Devil. He is Fellowship's 'true frende' (l. 212) and a lover of material Goods. Since his temptation and fall have been accomplished long before the summons of Death comes, the Vices are certain of his damnation. Goods, for example, replies to Everyman's profession of love by telling him, "That is to thy dampnancyon, without lesyne!" (l. 429) He is, of course, mistaken, for Everyman repents and receives mercy. Although the conflict of the Vices and the Virtues is seen from a different perspective, *Everyman* has the same action as the other early moralities. In both *Castell* and *Everyman* the Coming of Death is merely the motivation for the resolution of that action.

To say, then, as Bevington does, that "The MOST COMMON PLOT of these moralities. ...was that of an allegorical contest for the spiritual welfare of the mankind hero"[19] is misleading. For I believe that there is, as far as we know from these plays, only one action in the moralities: the conflict between the Vices and the Virtues for possession of mankind's soul.[20]

The morality didactic intention and action lead to a particular structure. If we exclude the homiletic addresses to the audience with which the plays begin and end, this structure falls into seven steps. In *Castell*, *Wisdom*, and *Mankind*, these steps are dramatically portrayed. In *Everyman*, however, the structure is elliptical, that is, three of the steps have been omitted; but their occurrence is presumed, and the action develops thereafter according to the same general pattern used in the other moralities.

The action of *Castell*, *Mankind*, and *Wisdom* begins with the introduction of the major vice figures, who reveal their evil natures and their aims to the audience. In *Castell*, for example, World is presented in all his pride:

---

[19] Bevington, p. 9. (emphasis mine).

[20] I have emphasized this point although several scholars, for example, Hardin Craig *(English Religious Drama*, p. 351) and Criezenach ("Early English Drama", p. 57) have stated there is only one action because so many scholars have commented upon the various 'actions' of the morality play.

> al a-bowtyn my bane is blowe,
> In euery cost I am knowe,
> I do men rawyn on ryche rowe
>     tyle þei be dyth to dethys dent. (ll. 166-69)

And Flesh reveals his narcissism and his selfishness. To satisfy himself he would willingly destroy mankind:

> I loue wel myn ese,
> In lustis me to plese;
> þou synne my sowle sese,
>     I ȝeue not a myth. (ll. 244-47)

The action of *Wisdom* begins with a monologue by Lucifer who describes his intentions to tempt mankind and so to bring about the soul's destruction. In *Mankind*, the Vices are introduced through a scene involving Mercy, the major virtue figure. Mischief appears, interrupts Mercy's admonition to the audience to avoid evil, mocks him, and blasphemes the *Bible*. Nought Now-a-days, and Newgyse, his fellow vices, then appear to taunt Mercy.

This introduction of the Vices at the beginning of the play has two purposes. First, it establishes the nature of the Vices so clearly that the audience is certain to remember what mankind forgets – that the Vices are his enemies and the potential destroyers of his soul. Second, it begins the action by establishing the Vices' intention to tempt mankind. Unlike the three plays discussed above, *Everyman* omits the introduction of the major vice figures. The reason is obvious: Everyman has already been tempted and has already fallen. The action begins, therefore, with God's indictment against Everyman, which motivates Death's summons.

In *Castell*, *Wisdom*, and *Mankind*, the mankind figure is introduced next. He is in a state of virtue, or as Ramsey calls it, 'The Stage of Innocence'.[21] In *Castell*, Mankind is shown to be well aware of the conflict between his sensual and spiritual natures. Though he wishes to be virtuous, he is torn between the two, for, as he says:

> I wolde be ryche in gret a-ray,
>     & fayn I wolde my sowle saue (ll. 378-79)

---

[21] Ramsey, p. clvi.

The hero of *Mankind* also realizes this conflict. He states:

> ...I haue my composycyon
> Of a body & of a soull, of condycyon contrarye (189-90)

but with the help of Mercy, he hopes to eschew vice. In *Wisdom*, Mind, Will, and Understanding believe themselves to be impervious to temptation and find God's laws, as Understanding says, to be "...swetter to me þan sawoure of þe rose". (l. 388) In these plays the mankind figure is shown to be potentially weak but spiritually worthy, since he wishes to avoid sin and follow virtue. In *Everyman*, of course, no such state of virtue is shown because Everyman has fallen before the play begins.

The third step in *Castell*, *Mankind*, and *Wisdom* consists of the temptation and the fall of the mankind figure, who chooses vice for several reasons. *Castell's* Mankind forgets that one never knows when death may come. He believes that he has time to pursue sensual pleasures and that he can repent of them later. He decides, therefore,

> ...with þe Werld I wyl go play,
> certis, a lytyle þrowe. (ll. 397-98)

for

> I may leuyn many a day;
> I am but ȝonge, as I trowe,
> for to do þat I schulde. (ll. 424-26)

The downfall of Mind, Will, and Understanding in *Wisdom* results from their inability to perceive that the arguments of Lucifer are specious. He convinces them that the contemplative life is not that of which God approves. Desiring to lead a virtuous life, the hero of *Mankind* seeks the counsel of Mercy. Mercy warns him to avoid Newgyse, Now-a-days, and Nought, and there seems to be no danger that Mankind will fall. Like Piers Plowman, he works in the earth, while the Vices stand about, trying to tempt him. Titivillus initiates Mankind's downfall by placing a board under the earth and by stealing a sack of corn. Unable to continue planting, Mankind becomes so angry that he forsakes his labor:

> Here I gyf wppe my spade, for now & for euer;
> To occupye my body, I wyll not put me in deuer (ll. 542-43)

This break in his habit of virtue leads him into a state of idleness; soon he breaks off a prayer because of Titivillus' tricks; and finally he gives up both:

> Of labure & preyer, I am nere yrke of both;
> I wyll no more of yt, thow Mercy be wroth! (ll. 578-79)

His downfall, then, results because he does not have the patience to endure the trials he faces. He simply gives up, although by doing so, he threatens his spiritual welfare and breaks faith with Mercy. Everyman's temptation is not part of the play. From the text, however, it is obvious that his fall resulted from his misplaced love and faith. Instead of placing his faith in God, he placed it in Fellowhip, where, as he says, "...is all myne affyaunce" (l. 199); and, as he tells Goods,

> ...thou hast had longe my hertely loue;
> I gaue the that whiche sholde be the Lordes aboue. (ll. 457-58)

As Ramsey has pointed out, the fourth step consists of mankind's life in sin[22] and is found in all four moralities. After he has fallen, the mankind figure accepts the seven deadly sins. The method of portraying this acceptance varies in each play. In *Castell*, the sins are allegorical figures whom Mankind meets once he has promised to serve the World. Lust and Folly array him so that he can be introduced to Couvetousness, Pride, Wrath, Envy, Lechery, Sloth and Gluttony. He greets them joyfully and accepts their counsels enthusiastically. In *Wisdom*, the vices which Mind, Will, and Understanding have embraced are made clear through the dialogue, and except for Lucifer no vice figure appears on stage. Understanding, for instance, is shown to be covetous:

> And my joy ys especially
> To hurd wppe ryches, from fer to fall,
> to se yt, to handyll yt, to tell yt all (ll. 584-86);

---

[22] *Ibid.*, p. clvi.

Will is lecherous: "And I, in lust my flesche to daunte" (l. 614); and Mind is proud: "Curyous a-ray I wyll euer hante." (l. 612) In *Mankind*, the hero's acceptance is indicated by his associates and his own actions. Mischief, Nought, Now-a-days, and Newgyse are so irreverent and foolish that Mankind's admiration for them proves that he is in a state of sin. Mankind's acceptance of the seven deadly sins is suggested, moreover, by his eagerness to go to a tavern and his lustful desire for a 'lemman'.[23] In *Everyman*, the hero's sinfulness is demonstrated by his companions and by the objects he cherishes. Fellowship, for example, helps to reveal Everyman's spiritual condition; for his willingness to join Everyman

> ...yf thou wylte ete & drynke & make good chere,
> Or haunt to women the lusty company (ll. 272–73)

suggests the gluttony and lust they have long pursued together. Everyman's protestations of love for Goods demonstrates his covetousness. The variations which the individual works display are of interest because they suggest that while the morality structure never alters, there is, nevertheless, some freedom within each step for the playwright to add whatever touches he wishes.

Mankind's life in sin is not dealt with very extensively in any of the moralities. In *Castell*, the hero meets the seven deadly sins and acknowledges his sinful condition:

> In sowre swetteness my syth I sende,
>   with seuene synnys sadde be-set.
> mekyl myrþe I moue in mynde,
>   with melody at my mowþis met (ll. 1243–46)

---

[23] The desire to go to a tavern and the desire for a 'lemman', like the change of garments, occur so frequently in moralities and moral interludes that they can be considered 'morality conventions'. From these comments and others made in this chapter, it is apparent that I disagree with C. F. Tucker Brooke's view that, 'Mankind' has as nearly as possible no plot; it touches no special part of the life of man, and it illustrates no truth of character or religion. Its comedy is perfectly devoid of intellectual interest..." *(The Tudor Drama*, p. 65). Like Sister Mary Philippa Coogan, I feel such comic scenes are of great importance because, "...they exemplify practically the teachings in the homiletic passages". *(An Interpretation of the Moral Play, Mankind*, Washington, D. C., The Catholic University Press, 1947, p. 93).

This speech climaxes the development of the first action (in *Castell*, there are two falls and two repentances). Soon afterwards, the Good Angel obtains the promises of Shift and Penance to lead Mankind to repentance. At first, he refuses to change, but finally he sighs for his sins and begs God's mercy. The life in sin of Mind, Will, and Understanding is dealt with in more detail. After they have turned from virtue, they justify their sinful life by attacking the values of the society in which they live. Understanding says, for example

> To be false, men report yt game;
> Yt is clepyde wysdom. (ll. 606-07)

The downfall of Mind, Will, and Understanding affects the moral condition of England and threatens the well-being of the nation. Mind becomes a maintainer of wrong and with his helpers seeks to destroy law reformers. Understanding forms a crew, the Holborn Quest, who, because they are the sons of Covetousness, will sell their verdicts for a bribe. Will has a crew of lecherous men. When Wisdom first appears, the three are irreverent; not until the disfigured Soul enters is there any indication that the three will repent. The extensive dialogue by Mind, Will, and Understanding regarding their plans for their life in sin deals with topical problems and attacks contemporary social evils. In this way, the work anticipates the 'social thesis play' which Louis B. Wright feels was developed in the Tudor moral interludes[24] and, moreover, anticipates the use of the morality pattern in those Tudor interludes concerned with the welfare of a state. In its social criticism, however, *Wisdom* differs from the other moralities discussed, going far beyond their scope.

In *Mankind*, the portrayal of the hero's life in sin is more limited. In a short scene, he is shown befriending Mischief, Now-a-days, and Nought, rejecting Mercy, and calling for a tapster. But during much of the period of his life in sin, he is not on stage at all. Instead Mercy laments Mankind's downfall while Mischief, Newgyse, Now-a-days, and Nought mock him. When Mankind next appears, he is almost in a state of despair because he perceives his sinfulness, and he soon repents.

---

[24] Louis B. Wright, "Social Aspects of Some Belated Moralities", *Anglia* (1930), 109. David Bevington discusses the play as satire in "Political Satire in the Morality *Wisdom Who Is Christ*". *Renaissance Papers, 1963*, 41-51.

Everyman is shown in the midst of his life in sin, but the dramatic emphasis is upon his discovery of its limitations. Less than halfway through the work, after he has realized that the love he gave Goods should have been given to God, Everyman begins his spiritual regeneration.

From a didactic point of view, the limited portrayal of mankind's life in sin is understandable. If this section were dwelled upon and particularly if it were made as merry as the mankind figures proclaim it to be, the exemplum would not serve its purpose adequately, since the joys rather than the sorrows of sin would be stressed. The structure, furthermore, develops the history of man's movement toward spiritual salvation, and his temptation and fall are but two parts of that history, the preludes to the more important steps of mankind's repentance and absolution. To limit the presentation of mankind's life in sin, therefore, is valid for both the didactic and the dramatic needs of the morality play.

*Castell*, the only play dealing with the entire scope of man's life, is the only one to have two falls and two repentances. These clarify the temptations which beset men at the beginning and the end of their lives. At the time of his first fall Mankind is very young, and it is not surprising that he would be tempted by the pleasures of the World, or that he would be unable to accept death as an imminent possibility. The ease with which he falls results from a natural desire to be "...a mery man on molde..." (l. 430). His second fall occurs when he is an old man. Mankind describes vividly the misery of age:

> I gynne to waxyn hory & colde;
> my bake gynnyth to bowe & bende;
> I crulle & crepe, & wax al colde;
> age makyth man ful vnthende,
>  body & bonys are febyl & sore. (ll. 2483-87)

As we might expect, he is not easily tempted, for the world offers him little. He leaves the Castle, where his 'best friends' are (l. 2518), only because he is beguiled by Covetousness. Poverty is fearful to the aged, for, as Covetousness correctly points out,

> if þou be pore, & nedy & elde,
>  þou schalt oftyn euyl fare. (ll. 2530-31)

Fearing such hardships, Mankind embraces Covetousness and so once again sacrifices his spiritual welfare for his physical comfort. The two falls give *Castell* psychological and theological depths which, at least for this writer, the other moralities do not have. Through the two falls, the conflict between the Vices and the Virtues is shown to be unending. The battle between the forces of good and evil which links the falls is, therefore, a brilliant stroke, a dramatization of the continuing struggle within Mankind himself.

In three moralities, the temptation to despair is the ultimate result of mankind's fall, and complete despair is the end which the Vices want to achieve. While Mind, Will, and Understanding are not tempted to despair, Lucifer makes it clear in his first monologue that he wishes to tempt mankind to do so:

> At hys deth I zall a-pere informable,
> Schewynge hym all hys synnys abhomynable,
> Prowynge hys soule damnable,
> So with dyspeyer I xall hym qwell. (ll. 540-43)

In *Castell*, the repentant and dying Mankind fights this last temptation, as he prays, "God keep me from dyspayr!" (l. 2991) The hero of *Mankind*, so close to despair that he almost commits suicide, fears that he is unworthy of forgiveness because of his life in sin. As he tells Mercy,

> Alasse! I haue be so bestyally dysposyde, I dare not a-pere.
> To se yowur solaycyose face, I am not worthy to dysyer. (ll. 806-07)

Everyman, too, almost despairs after his conversation with Goods:

> For my Goodes sharpely dyd me tell
> That he bryngeth many in to hell.
> Than of my selfe I was ashamed,
> And so I am worthy to be blamed;
> Thus may I well my self hate. (ll. 474-78)

If the mankind figures did succumb to despair, they would certainly be damned, and the Vices would, then, vanquish the Virtues. As Eleanor Prosser states,

## 56 THE MORALITY PATTERN, A DEFINITION

...the orthodox concept of despair is of great importance for both medieval and Renaissance drama. ...We tend to forget that within the Christian tradition despair was (and is) the most heinous of sins, a sin against the Holy Ghost.[25]

Since the moralities seek to turn men to virtuous living, it is part of their didactic purpose to point out: "...that no sin is too great to be forgiven if the sinner has faith".[26] Consequently, no matter how close they may come to it, the mankind figures never succumb fully to despair. The temptation to do so provides the transition from mankind's life in sin to his repentance.

Repentance depends upon the correction of mankind's spiritual vision. In *Castell*, immediately before his second repentance, Mankind is faced with the actuality of death. He turns to World, seeking his help. World not only refuses to help him, but, furthermore, reveals his true nature:

> oure bonde of loue schal sone be broke;
> In colde clay schal be þy cage;
> now schal þe Werld on þee be wroke,
> for þou hast don so gret outrage;
> þi good þou schalt for-goo.
> Werldlys good þou hast for-gon,
> & with tottys þou schalt be torn:
> þus haue I seruyd here be-forn,
> a hundryd thousand moo. (ll. 2874-82)

Because World and Covetousness take off their masks, Mankind finally sees them as they are, not as they appeared to be. Having seen them truly, he wishes, of course, to turn from them. The harshness of World's speech, then, contributes to Mankind's repentance, despite the fact that World's intention is the very opposite, to bring Mankind to despair. In *Everyman*, repentance is brought about in the same way. Goods destroys Everyman's illusions by destroying bluntly his assumptions about Goods himself. In *Wisdom*, repentance is brought about because Wisdom (Christ) admonishes the Soul. Again, the mankind figure is forced to see truly, in this instance, to see himself as he is:

---

[25] Eleanor Prosser, *Drama and Religion in the English Mystery Plays* ("Stanford Studies in Language and Literature", Vol. XXIII; Stanford, Stanford University Press, 1961), p. 32.
[26] *Ibid*. p. 33.

> As many dedly synnys as ye haue vsyde,
> So many deullys in yowur soule be.
> Behold what ys þer-in reclusyde!
> Alas, man! of þi soule haue pyte! (ll. 913-16)

The Soul, of course, turns in shame from the Vice he had embraced. In *Mankind* the reason for the hero's repentance is omitted. Although Mankind enters in a desperate state, how he has reached this state is never known. But as in the other moralities, so in *Mankind*, repentance is the ultimate result of the hero's corrected vision.

Repentance consists of the four traditional elements, faith, contrition, confession, and penance, although the last may not be dramatically portrayed. The mankind figures all realize that God is merciful to the repentant sinner. In *Castell*, dying Mankind knows that his sins will surely damn his soul unless "God me graunte of his grace".. (l. 3003) His Soul calls upon Mercy, who, with Peace, pleads for his salvation before God. In *Wisdom*, Understanding implies his faith in divine mercy when he suggests that Mind and Will return with him to God, Who "...ys resurreccion & lywe to hem wyll resort". (l. 944) Will agrees, believing that God

> ...of hys mercy, he wyll me able
> to haue þe yiffte of hys specyall grace. (ll. 950-51)

The Soul then prays for divine forgiveness. When he realizes that his book of good works is empty, Everyman begs for Jesus' help. Knowledge takes him to Confession, who promises Everyman that if

> ...ye wyll saued be,
> Aske God Mercy, and he wyll graunte truely. (ll. 569-70)

The last section of *Mankind* is devoted almost completely to establishing that God is merciful rather than just to the repentant sinner. Mercy assures despondent Mankind that on Judgment Day, he "...schall rewle þe mater with-owte controuersye". (l. 835)

In all four moralities, contrition is indicated by the mankind figure's awareness of his sinfulness. In *Castell*, Mankind's first repentance follows the traditional form: he is contrite, he confesses, and he does penance.[27] His second repentance, however, is less clearly developed. His contrition is shown by his lamentations:

> now, alas, my lyf is lak;
>    bitter balys I gynne to brewe;
> Certis, a vers þat Dauid spak
> I þe sawter, I fynde it trewe:
>    Tesauriȝat, & ignorat cui congreabit ea. (ll. 2983–86)

His confession takes the form of an address to the audience:

> now, good men, takythe example at me!
>    do for ȝoure self whyl ȝe han spase!
> for many men pus seruyd be,
>    þorwe þe Werld, in dyuerse place.
> I bolne & bleyke in blody ble,
>    & as a flour, fadyth my face. (ll. 2996–3000)

His penance is not portrayed but it is implied. Although the Soul calls upon Mercy, the Bad Angel takes it to Hell, where it remains until it has cleansed itself and until God offers Mankind divine grace. In *Wisdom*, Christ informs the Soul that the first stage of repentance is contrition, which, "...with confession and satisfaction cleanse the soul". (l. 124) Once the Soul begins to weep for her sins, the devils which plagued her withdraw. She assures Christ that,

> With wepynge ey, & hert contryte,
> To owur modyr, holy chyrche, I will resort,
> My lyff pleyn schewenge to here syght,
> With mynde, understondyne, & will ryght. (ll. 994–97)

Contrite, she promises to confess. Her penance is not shown. *Mankind*'s hero is contrite and confesses his sins, but he fears, at first, that he will not be absolved:

> yt ys so abhomminabell to rehers my werst transgrescion;
>    I am not worthy to hawe mercy, be no possibilite. (ll. 814–15)

He does no penance. Knowledge leads Everyman to Confession, from whom he receives

---

[27] Miss Prosser has an excellent discussion of repentance; *ibid.*, pp. 33–37.

> ...that scourge of me,
> Whiche is penaunce stronge that ye must endure,
> To remembre thy Sauyour was scourged for the
> With sharpe scourges, and suffred it pacyently (ll. 561-64)

Contrition is demonstrated by Everyman's regret for his misplaced love, and it becomes a part of him, symbolized by the robe of contrition he wears.

The seventh and last step consists of mankind's absolution. In *Castell*, it occurs after the Soul has suffered for its sins. Once God has forgiven Mankind, his soul is permitted to enter Heaven. In *Wisdom*, absolution occurs after the Soul has promised Christ that she will do penance. He tells her:

> Now ye haue for-sake synne, & be contryte,
> Ye were neuer so leve to me verelye;
> Now be ye reformyde to yowur bewtys bryght. (ll. 1094-96)

Everyman's absolution is achieved when an Angel welcomes him to Heaven, "Come, excellente electe spouse to Iesu!" (l. 894) The four moralities end happily, therefore, because the mankind figures receive mercy. In *Castell* and *Everyman* they literally attain Heaven. In *Wisdom*, the Soul is at peace with God; in *Mankind*, the hero is warned to avoid his enemies and free to return to the virtuous life he had pursued formerly. At the conclusion of each play, forgiven and regenerate mankind is in a state of virtue, and presumably in *Wisdom* and *Mankind*, he will, thereafter, lead a godly life.

The problem of mankind's spiritual vision is central to the development of the morality structure. In each play, mankind's fall is the result of his clouded reason, of a wrong choice brought about by incorrect perceptions, leading him to incorrect judgments. The argument of Lucifer in *Wisdom*, for example, is clearly fallacious:

> The wyll of þe soule hath fre dominacion;
> Dyspute not to moche in þis with reson (ll. 481-82);

and it contradicts Christ's:

> No thyne xulde offende Gode in no kynde;
> Ande yff þer does þat, þe nether parte of reasone
> In no wys þer-to lende;
> Than þe ouer parte xall haue fre domynacion. (ll. 297-300)

In *Castell*, once Mankind has chosen the joys of sensual life over those of spiritual life, he completely inverts his values. As he says:

> I wolde be ryche & of gret renoun.
> [Of God] Iʒeue no tale trewly,
>   So þat I be lord of toure & toun,
>     be buskys & bankys broun. (ll. 571-74)

The hero of *Mankind*, who previously had ignored Newgyse, Now-a-days, and Nought, embraces them and ironically begs, "I crye you mercy of all þat I dyde a-mysse." (l. 651) Once mankind has assented to vice, he is spiritually blind, and he cannot evaluate correctly the information his senses bring him. He has cut himself off from Wisdom and Light;[28] left to himself, he can only continue in the darkness of his lower, sensual nature. *Everyman* presents the result of man's life in sin, the final awareness that all he sought is paltry. The repentance of Everyman comes after his 'education to spiritual rejuvenation' has corrected his perception.[29] As has been discussed above, the mankind figure is incapable of regeneration until his spiritual vision has been corrected, until he recognizes the Vices for the evil forces they are and until he recognizes the sinful life he has been living. Mankind's fall and regeneration, therefore, depend to a large extent upon the clarity of his spiritual vision.

The characters in these English moralities can be separated into three definite groups: the mankind figure, the virtue figures, and the vice figures. All three are dramatic personifications of moral positions in a Christian universe.

The hero of the morality is the mankind figure, whose soul is the object for which the Vices and the Virtues struggle. In *Castell*, *Mankind*, and *Everyman*, as his name proves, he is meant to represent typical Christian man, after the Fall, who has within him the potential for good or evil. In *Castell* we know nothing about Mankind's earthly life which would distinguish him from other men, and there is no attempt to limit this characterization by particularizing him or his life in any way. In *Mankind* and *Everyman*, on the other hand, while the characterizations are still gener-

---

[28] See *Wisdom* for a summary of the theological relationship between Wisdom (Christ) and Light, ll. 20-25.

[29] Ryan, pp. 725-29.

alized, there is an inchoate tendency to particularize the heroes. Mankind is a farmer, albeit one reminiscent of Piers Plowman, and the temptations he undergoes are suited to this particular station. *Everyman* is limited to a particular time in the life of the mankind figure. The hero, neither king nor beggar, is an adult, old enough to have devoted his life to Fellowship and Goods. The particularization of Mankind and Everyman is, on the whole, slight, and, consequently, of relative unimportance to this discussion. It does, however, suggest a tendency which will be demonstrated in the Tudor moral interludes: the tendency to individualize a generalized mankind figure so that he becomes a particular person, living in a particular time and place.

Unlike these plays, *Wisdom* does not employ a single mankind figure who represents typical humanity. Instead, personifications of the divisions of the human soul are used, but they function precisely as do Mankind and Everyman. The use of such personifications and the division of a mankind figure into three separate dramatic characters illustrate tendencies which occur in later drama. Occasionally, personifications in the Tudor moral interludes function as mankind figures. More important, in some Tudor moral interludes and some Renaissance comedies, the number of mankind figures is increased so that several and varying types of humanity are presented.

The mankind figure is dynamic in the sense that his personality changes as his spiritual condition changes. At the beginning of the action, that is, before he is tempted, he reveals his middle position between good and evil and the conflict between his spiritual and sensual natures. Once he falls, he exhibits an excessive love for the things of the world, and he embraces the seven deadly sins. When his repentance begins, his character alters. He becomes the sorrowful soul, contrite humanity, confessing his crimes against God and concerned only about his spiritual welfare. At last, he becomes the regenerate Christian, for whom the world is but a preparation for the eternal life of his soul.

The Virtues and the Vices are static characters; that is, they remain what they always were and undergo no change. The Virtues are the forces of good; they seek mankind's spiritual well-being and the salvation of his soul. The Vices are their antithesis, the forces of evil which tempt mankind to spiritual damnation. Their natures are contrasted by their attitudes toward Mankind's spiritual predicament. The Virtues find it a matter of utmost importance. They are constantly teaching mankind, and through him the members of the audience, how to avoid sin. Mercy, for example, begins *Mankind* with an exhortation to the audience on the need for concern about one's spiritual welfare and ends it with a sermon, addressed to the hero, on repentant man's potential for divine forgiveness. The Vices, on the other hand, are shown to be either unconcerned about mankind's predicament or bent upon destroying his soul. In *Castell*, for instance, Flesh seeks to satisfy his every whim and would willingly destroy mankind if necessary in order to do so. Most Vices, of course, are actively mankind's enemy. *Castell*'s World, *Wisdom*'s Lucifer, and *Everyman*'s Goods, to name but three, make it all too clear that their aim is mankind's damnation.

A summary of the elements isolated and discussed in this chapter provides a definition of the early English morality play. The morality is a dramatized allegory based upon Christian dogma, written for a Christian audience. It has a single didactic intention: to lead the members of the audience to eschew vice, repent their sins, and embrace virtue so that they may win the salvation of their souls. This intention is explicit, and each play opens and closes with a statement of the theological concepts it dramatizes.

The morality has a single action and a single outcome. The action centers in the conflict between the Virtues and the Vices for the soul of mankind. It ends with the Virtues victorious, the Vices defeated, and repentant mankind absolved of sin by God's mercy. If we exclude the address to the audience which frames the action, the structure falls into seven steps: the introduction of the vice figures; the introduction of the mankind figure in a state of virtue; his temptation and fall; his life in sin; the temptation to give way to despair, which forms a transition from mankind's life in sin to his repentance; his repentance, consisting of faith, contrition, confession, and penance; and, finally, mankind's absolution through divine mercy. Central to the structure is the problem of mankind's spiritual vision. Because his vision is clouded, he is tempted by the apparent rather than the real good. Once he has fallen, mankind is blind to the nature of the vices he embraces and blind to his own spiritual condition. His spiritual vision begins to be corrected once he recognizes the Vices for what they are: the potential destroyers of his soul. But until he recognizes that he need not despair because of his sins, until he has faith that God, out of His infinite mercy, will forgive the repentant sinner, his vision is not totally clear. Repentant mankind sees clearly what he should avoid and what he should embrace. Having been absolved, he will, presumably, live a godly life and be blind no more to the nature of evil.

Every morality contains three character types, all personifying moral positions in a Christian universe. The Vices are those who struggle with the Virtues to win possession of mankind's soul. They represent the forces of evil, against which mankind must guard. The Virtues are the forces of good, which attempt to turn mankind from sin and help him achieve salvation. The mankind figure represents typical Christian humanity, torn between his sensual and spiritual natures. Though he falls into a life of sin, with the help of the Virtues, he is capable of regeneration. Regenerate mankind, forgiven his trespasses, exemplifies both the potentiality of all Christian men and the benevolence of a merciful God. By watching his struggles and his spiritual victory, the members of the audience learn that they, too, can achieve what he has achieved and receive the mercy he has received.

A comparison of the elements isolated in the morality play and those elements in *How a Man May Chuse* which separate it from other types of comedy shows that this Renaissance play shares most of its distinguishing characteristics with the morality. It, too, is based upon orthodox Christian dogma and has, as Arthur's concluding address illustrates, the explicit didactic intention of teaching the members of the audience the means to spiritual salvation. Since on a moral level, Mistress Arthur and Mary represent opposing forces of good and evil, we can say that the former has the aim and function of a virtue figure, while the latter has the aim and function of a vice figure. Young Arthur, standing between them, with the potential for either good or evil, is clearly a typical mankind figure. The action and structure of *How a Man May Chuse* follow those of the morality closely. Certainly, Mistress Arthur and Mary, that is, Virtue and Vice, struggle for possession of Young Arthur's soul, and, as in the moralities, the Vice is defeated. The play begins, as does *Everyman*, with the mankind figure in the midst of his life in sin. But Old Arthur's comments about his son's previous state of virtue recall the first three steps of the morality structure. Arthur is tempted to despair; he repents, that is, his faith is restored, he is contrite, he confesses his sins, and he does penance; and, finally, he is forgiven his crimes just as the mankind figures are absolved of their sins.

The similarities between the morality and *How a Man May Chuse* demonstrate the validity of the hypothesis upon which this study is based. This type of Renaissance play cannot be placed in traditional comic sub-genres. It belongs, therefore, to another category. And since its major distinguishing elements are those isolated in the morality play, *How a Man May Chuse* should be considered an example of the Renaissance morality-patterned comedy.

III

# EVOLUTION, AS REFLECTED IN SOME TUDOR MORAL INTERLUDES

The development of the morality-patterned comedy can be suggested best by an examination of selected Tudor moral interludes, those allegorical plays employing the morality elements defined in Chapter II.[1] The discovery of how these interludes differ from the older moralities should provide clues to the evolution from morality play to the morality-patterned comedy of the Renaissance.

[1] After careful consideration, a number of Tudor interludes have been eliminated from this chapter for various reasons. Since the chapter investigates a line of descent, there has been no attempt to study Tudor interludes fully, a task requiring a full-length work. The extant works of John Bale have been excluded because some, for example, *God's Promises* (1538) and *The Temptation of Our Lord and Saviour Jesus Christ by Satan* (1538), are mysteries; the *Three Laws of Nature, Moses, and Christ* (1538) does not contain 'mankind figures' as the term has been defined in Chapter II; and *King Johan* (c. 1538, A-version) alters the morality structure. Lewis Wager's *The Life and Repentance of Mary Magdalene* (c. 1550-1566) has been excluded because, in my opinion, it is primarily a miracle play, employing some morality elements. Other interludes have been omitted for any one of the following reasons: 1) they have no 'mankind figure' as the term was defined above; 2) they vary the morality structure so that the play ends tragically; 3) they are so loosely developed that I felt they could not properly be considered to use the full morality structure. These include *Godly Queen Hester* (1525-1529); the plays of W. Wager, *The Longer Thou Livest, The More Foole Thou Art* (c. 1559-1568), *Enough Is As Good As a Feast* (c. 1559-1570), and *The Trial of Treasure* (?, published 1567); Ulpian Fulwell's *Like Will to Like* (1562-1568); Thomas Lupton's *All for Money* (1559-1577); Thomas Garter's *The Most Virtuous and Godly Susanna* (1563-1569); John Pickering's *The Interlude of Vice (Horestes)* (1567); George Walpull's *The Tyde Tarrieth No Man* (published 1576); and Robert Wilson's *The Three Ladies of London* (c. 1581). *Nice Wanton* (1547-1553), Thomas Ingelend's *The Disobedient Child* (c. 1559-1570), and George Gascoigne's *The Glasse of Government*, none of which are completely allegorical and all of which are traditionally considered English examples of 'education drama', are discussed in the Appendix.

The works considered begin at the end of the fifteenth century and end at the beginning of the seventeenth, so that they overlap slightly into the period of morality-patterned comedies. My method is descriptive. What happens, not why, is the only concern of this chapter, and there is no attempt to deal with theological, social, or intellectual backgrounds. Since a completely chronological discussion would lead to unnecessary repetition, the interludes have been grouped according to themes in order to clarify the changes which occur in the morality pattern. Within the groups, however, the discussions are chronological. The emphasis in each is the same: to compare and contrast these Tudor moral interludes with the older moralities, and, in this way, to point out the changes affecting the development of the morality-patterned comedy.

As we shall see, these allegorical Tudor moral interludes have in general the same didactic intention, action, structure, and character types as the older morality plays. But the structural development becomes somewhat looser. The first step, the introduction of the major vice figures, is sometimes omitted. The repentance of the mankind figure is often presented in less detail, while his life in sin is often presented in greater detail than it was in the older moralities. A tendency to particularize the action occurs in most interludes. The mankind figure rarely remains abstract everyman; he becomes, instead, a type, perhaps, mankind the youth, mankind the student, or mankind the king. While the conflict between the Vices and the Virtues for possession of mankind's soul occurs in these interludes, it is developed within a particular context, possibly one having to do with the welfare of the state, the education of youth, or the proper control of wealth. The action, moreover, is extended beyond the scope of the older moralities. The mankind figure struggles not only for his spiritual salvation, but for his worldly reputation and success as well. For in accordance with the Renaissance concern about man's earthly life, these Tudor moral interludes become exempla teaching men how to achieve both spiritual salvation and earthly happiness.

*Nature* (c. 1490–c. 1501) and *Mundus et Infans* (c. 1500–1522) are the only interludes to deal, as does *The Castell of Perseverance*, with the full range of mankind's earthly life. As we shall discover, the others are limited to one specific incident.

Henry Medwall's *Nature*, which is in two parts, begins with the Vices and the Virtues sitting together on the stage while Nature, the major virtue figure, instructs Mankind, and through him the audience, concerning her role, and her relationship to God. She states, as well, the play's didactic intention:

> ...to put thee [man] in knowledge and memory
> To what intent thou art ordained to be here.[2]

Mankind, a youth, shows that he is well aware of his place in the scheme of things:

> ... Thou hast given me virtue
> Surmounting all other in high perfection:
> ... Yet, for all that, have I free election
> [To] do what I will, be it evil or well;
> And am put in the hand of mine own counsel. (p. 47)

Though he wishes to live virtuously, he fails to do so because he is beguiled by the fallacious arguments of the World, who tells him one

> ... must needs do as the world doth
> That intendeth any while here to reign;
> And follow the guise that now-a-day goeth,
> As far as his estate may it maintain.
> And who doth the contrary – I will be plain–
> He is abject and despised utterly. (p. 57)

Following World's counsel, Mankind rejects the Virtue Innocence and embraces the Vice Worldly Affection. Blind to their natures, he accepts as well the Seven Deadly Sins as the friends they purport to be, believing, to name but three, that Pride is Worship; Covetousness, Worldly Policy; and Wrath, Manhood. Part I ends with Mankind's recognition of his sins, his first repentance, and his forgiveness.

Part II deals with Mankind's second fall and repentance in old age. Although he falls because he is tempted by lust, eventually, as for *Castell*'s hero, covetousness becomes Mankind's greatest sin.

---

[2] Henry Medwall, *Nature*, in *Recently Recovered "Lost" Tudor Plays with Some Others*, edited by John S. Farmer (London, Early English Drama Society, 1907), p. 43. Other references to the play will be made in the body of the text.

His second repentance follows the traditional morality pattern. Realizing that he deserves no 'meed' for his sins, Mankind is saved from the temptation to despair by Reason, who restores his faith in divine mercy. Contrite, he confesses his sins. His penance, however, is not portrayed; instead, following the counsel of Reason, he replaces the sins with their equivalent virtues: Meekness, Charity, Patience, Good Occupation, Liberality, Abstinence, and Chastity, who teach him how to eschew vice and achieve spiritual salvation. At the end, regenerate Mankind has certainly been forgiven. As Reason tells him, he is

> ... fully the child of salvation.
> Have good perseverance, and be not in fear;
> Thy ghostly enemy can put thee in no danger. (p. 133)

As this brief summary indicates, *Nature* is very similar to the morality plays discussed in Chapter II. There is, however, one change which is important in our examination of the Tudor interlude. Pearl Hogrefe points out that the play reveals "...a freshness in the appreciation of natural beauty..." and that "...English morality plays such as *Everyman* and *The Castell of Perseverance* lack the freshness of detail in these lines from Medwall's *Nature*:

> Who taught the cok hys watche howers to observe
> And syng of corage wyth shryll throte on hye,
> Who taught the pelly can her tender hart to carue
> For she nolde suffer her byrdys to dye.
> Who taught the nyghtyngall to recorde besyly
> Her straunge entunys in sylence of the nyght?
> Certes I nature and none other syght. (I, 43-49)"[3]

Such freshness indicates a tendency more fully developed in later Tudor moral interludes: the tendency toward greater particularization, reflected here in the use of realistic details.

The anonymous *Mundus et Infans* begins at the moment of mankind's birth and ends in his old age. The statement of didactic intention having been omitted, the play opens with the introduction of World, the major vice figure, whose first speech establishes his excessive pride. He tells the audience:

---

[3] Pearl Hogrefe, *The Sir Thomas More Circle* (Urbana, The University of Illinois Press, 1959), pp. 259-260. Miss Hogrefe points out, moreover, the originality in Medwall's concept of the goddess Nature (pp. 260-261). Her discussion of Nature has, I feel, no relevance to this study.

> ... I am ruler of realmes, I warne you all,
> And ouer all fodys I am kynge,
> For I am kynge well knowen in these realmes rounde.[4]

Infans, the mankind figure, is then introduced, complaining, as does *Castell's* Mankind, of his wretchedness:

> Now in to the Worlde she hathe me sent,
> Poore and naked as ye may see;
> I am not worthely wrapped nor went,
> But powerly prycked in pouerte. (ll. 44-47)

While recognizing that man's earthly life is but the passage to the eternal life of his soul, Infans succumbs swiftly to the temptations of the world. As though he acted in the only manner possible for any man, he turns to Mundus for sensual comfort and accepts the Vice without considering even for a moment the spiritual significance of his act. At that age, he first meets Conscience, who persuades him that the vices he has embraced threaten his spiritual well-being. Infans seems about to amend, for he promises Conscience that he will turn from these vices. But this promise is soon broken; he is incapable of forsaking the World, because "... mankynde he doth mery make" (l. 507), and unwilling to sacrifice his temporal comforts for his spiritual good. His regeneration does not occur until he has reached old age. Having finally recognized the Vices to be his spiritual enemies and ashamed of his life in sin, Infans almost despairs of forgiveness. Fortunately, he meets Perseverance, who listens to his confession and restores his faith in divine mercy by assuring him that

> ... Ye are possyble heuen to wynne,
> But with grete contrycyon ye must begynne,
> And take you to abstynence. (ll. 858-61)

That Infans has obtained forgiveness is suggested by Perseverance who names him,

> ... Repentaunce,
> Throughe the grace of God Almyght. (ll. 974-75)

---

[4] *Mundus et Infans*, in *Specimens of the Pre-Shakespearean Drama*, edited by John Matthews Manly (Boston, Ginn and Company, 1897), I, ll. 3-5. Other references to the play will be made in the body of the text.

The moral significance of the play is indicated by the regenerate Infans, who tells the audience: "Now, syrs, take all ensample by me." (l. 966)

While *Mundus et Infans* employs most morality elements and follows the morality structure, there are two differences worthy of note. The statement of didactic purpose with which the moralities begin is omitted. More important, however, is the fact that mankind's life in sin, which receives much less attention in the older moralities, takes up more than half of this play. The stages of man's life in sin are revealed through the maturing of Infans, who at seven becomes 'Wanton', at fourteen 'Lust-and-Lyking', at nineteen 'Mankind', and finally 'Age'. Each stage stresses the vices appropriate to a sinful man at a particular time in his life. Wanton, for example, is the naughty child who fights with his siblings and disobeys his parents. As the name indicates, Lust-and-Lyking is a lustful youth; Manhood is bloated with pride; and Age is the culmination of a life in sin, despairing man, bereft of worldly goods and fearful of spiritual damnation. The expansion of mankind's life in sin in this play serves to emphasize man's frailty rather than his potential for spiritual salvation and, consequently, provides a more detailed examination than that found in the older moralities of the sins to which each age is prone.

*Nature* and *Mundus et Infans* are the only Tudor moral interludes to deal with man's complete earthly life. In the remaining plays to be discussed, the action is always limited in some way. It may be limited by the particular age of the mankind figure and concerned only with the problems appropriate to that age. Or it may deal with a particular contemporary social problem such as that of education, the control of wealth, or civil responsibilities. As E. K. Chambers says, the dramatists of the Tudor moral interludes

> ...make their selection from amongst the battalions of sins and virtues which were to invade the stage together and set themselves the task of expounding the dangers of a particular temperament or the advantages of a particular form of moral discipline.[5]

The limitation of the morality pattern has, of course, precedent in the older moralities. Except for *The Castell of Perseverance* the

---

[5] E. K. Chambers, *The Mediaeval Stage* (London, Oxford University Press, 1903), II, 200.

moralities are limited to one situation, the hero of *Mankind* is a farmer, and the action of *Everyman* takes place shortly before the hero's death. None of these plays, however, particularizes as fully as those works to be discussed.

*Hyckescorner* (c. 1513-1516) employs a single but generalized situation. Like the mankind figures in *Wisdom*, those in *Hyckescorner* are not meant to represent general humanity; they are, instead, allegorical personifications of human characteristics, specifically Freewill and Imagination. Pity, as his name indicates, is the major virtue character. He begins the play by introducing himself and suggesting the play's didactic function: "Who-so me loveth damned never shall be."[6] Perseverance and Contemplation enter, and the three complain about the immoral condition of England. Freewill and Imagination are then introduced in the midst of their lives in sin. They call for Hyckescorner, who, I believe, represents the Vice of Impiety. As his tale of a shipwreck in which Virtues were drowned and Vices saved demonstrates, he delights in the triumph of evil over good. Like all Vices, he attempts to defeat the Virtues which threaten him. Consequently, he advises Freewill and Imagination to attack Pity because, "He wolde destroye us all, and all our kynne!" (l. 499) Once Pity has been bound, Hyckescorner leaves with Freewill and Imagination, never to reappear. Although his sudden disappearance from the play is dramatically weak, it does have some structural justification. Immediately afterwards Contemplation and Perseverance enter, release Pity, and decide to bring about the repentance of Freewill and Imagination. They finally succeed. The mankind figures do not fight the temptation to despair, but, contrite for their sins, they confess and beg divine forgiveness:

    Frewyll. Now of all my synnes I axe God mercy;
    Here I forsake synne and trust to amend. (ll. 865-66)
    . . . . . . . . . . . . . . . . . . .
    Mag. No-thynge dred I so sore as deth;
    There fore to amende I thynke hyt be tyme.
    Synne have I used all the days of my breth,
    . . . Here of all my synnes I axe God mercy. (ll. 994-96, 99)

---

[6] *Hyckescorner*, in *Specimens of the Pre-Shakespearean Drama*, I, l. 26. Other references to the play will be made in the body of the text.

No penance is indicated. That Freewill and Imagination have been forgiven, however, is clear, since, after they have repented, their functions change. Freewill, who can serve either good or evil, attaches himself to Perseverance. Imagination becomes Good Remembrance and attaches himself to Contemplation. Perseverance ends the play with an address to the audience, counselling them to remember Repentance and to think upon their heavenly rewards.

While the play follows the morality pattern, it suggests trends which are developed more fully in other interludes. Despite the generalized characters and the generalized incident, there are frequent topical references to such places as 'Newgate' and 'Holborn' and to such contemporary conditions as:

> Youth walketh by nyght with swerdes and knyves,
> And, ever amonge, true men leseth theyr lyves. (ll. 561-62)

As contrasted with the older moralities, these references indicate the tendency of the Tudor moral interludes to particularize and, especially, to place a work within a contemporary framework so that is deals with contemporary social problems. The morality structure, furthermore, is extremely loose: the introduction of the vices, the first step in the moralities, is omitted; mankind's life in sin is expanded enormously; and mankind's repentance is contracted greatly. Because of these structural variations, *Hyckescorner* suggests the tendency, which occurs as well in other interludes, to manipulate the structural elements of the older morality while following the overall structural pattern.

*Youth* (1513-1529) limits the action, as the title suggests, by restricting the age of the mankind figure. As we might expect, the young man at first refuses, "In my youth to lose my jollity",[7] and, consequently, ignores the advice of Charity, who seeks to turn him toward a more virtuous but less merry life. He chooses, instead, to follow Riot. He takes Pride as his servant and Lecchery as his 'lemman', vices appropriate for a young man. Most of the play deals with Youth's life in sin, developed largely through Charity's attempts to turn him from it and his willful refusal to abandon the vices he has embraced. Although he does not struggle

---

[7] *The Interlude of Youth* in *A Select Collection of Old English Plays*, edited by W. Carew Hazlitt (4th ed.; London, Reeves and Turner, 1874), II, ll. Other references to the play will be made in the body of the text.

with the temptation to despair, Youth does, nevertheless, finally repent. His sorrow for his sins, his confession, and his faith in divine mercy are suggested by his statement:

> Here all sin I forsake,
> And to God I me betake;
> Good Lord, I pray thee have no indignation,
> That I, a sinner, should ask salvation. (p. 37)

Having eschewed the vices he had embraced, Youth becomes Good Contrition, who promises that,

> For my sin I will mourn,
> All creatures I will turn;
> And when I see misdoing men,
> Good counsel I shall give them,
> And exhort them to amend. (p. 39)

While *Youth* exemplifies one method by which the Tudor moral interlude might be particularized, it is less interesting and fruitful for this discussion than those plays which do so by using the morality pattern to expound a particular topic.

*Lusty Juventus* (1547-53), for example, is limited by its involvement in the Reformation, in the controversy between Catholicism and Protestantism. The play's didactic intention, stated at the beginning and at the end of the work, is to teach the members of the audience

> ... hypocrisy to know,
> With which the devil, as with a poison most pestilent,
> Daily seeketh all men to overthrow.[8]

and, especially, to teach the young to "Set your delight both day and night on Christ's testament". (p. 100) It achieves its purpose by attacking Catholicism and by showing the evil results of sensuality. While their elders practice Catholicism and thus serve Satan, the young,

> ... will not believe, they plainly say,
> In old traditions and made by men,
> But they will live, as the Scripture teacheth them. (p. 62)

---

[8] R. Wever, *Lusty Juventus*, in *A Select Collection of Old English Plays*, II, 99-100. Other references to the play will be made in the body of the text.

The youth have escaped the snares of a false creed. Satan offers them in its place sensual temptation, which, like Catholicism, would bring about their spiritual damnation.

The play opens with Juventus, the young mankind figure, totally unconcerned about his spiritual welfare. He meets Good Counsel, who soon convinces him that he ought to be concerned and who, with the help of Knowledge, explains Protestant dogma to him. Juventus, as a result, becomes a 'New Gospeller'. To draw the youth from virtuous living and so to win his soul, the Devil orders Hypocrisy to bring about his downfall. Disguised as Friendship, Hypocrisy becomes the boy's companion and introduces him to Wicked Fellowship and Abhominable Living. Juventus' spiritual vision is weak, for he does not recognize the Vices as his enemies but thinks them the friends they appear to be. He falls into a life of sin, which he pursues until Counsel reminds him of his potential damnation. Perceiving his errors, Juventus almost despairs, because, "To ask for mercy now, I know, it is too late." (p. 95) Counsel and Merciful Promise, however, convince him that God forgives the repentant sinner. Contrite, he confesses his sins, but he does no penance. The regenerate and forgiven Juventus sums up the moral significance of the interlude for the audience, counselling them to learn from him to recognize the hypocritical followers of Satan and to eschew vice and embrace virtue.

This brief summary of *Lusty Juventus* demonstrates what becomes increasingly obvious in an examination of these Tudor moral interludes: the morality pattern proves to be extremely flexible. It provides the playwright with his major dramatic organization, while, at the same time, it is capable of whatever minor variations are necessary to accomodate an interlude's specific concern.

Man's need for education is the subject of two plays, John Rastell's *The Nature of the Four Elements* (c. 1517–1518), also called *The Interlude of the Four Elements*, and John Redford's *Wyt and Science* (1531–1547). In both, the problem of man's education is fused with the problem of his spiritual salvation.

The purpose of *The Four Elements* is to demonstrate that man must know "... God's creatures that be..."[9] if he is to obtain a true knowledge of God; for

[9] John Rastell, *The Interlude of the Four Elements*, in *A Select Collection of Old English Plays*, I, 7. Other references to the play will be made in the body of the text.

> How dare men presume to be called clerks,
> Disputing of high creatures celestial,
> As things invisible and God's high warks,
> And know not these visible things inferial? (p. 9)

The play's didactic intention, therefore, is two-fold: to illustrate man's need to learn about the natural world and to teach man how he may work toward his spiritual salvation. Since knowledge of God depends upon knowledge of the natural world and since it is necessary for man's spiritual welfare, knowledge of the natural world must be one means by which man works toward the salvation of his soul.

Instruction about the natural world takes up much of the play's space and in the prologue brings a plea for more books written in the vernacular:

> For though many make books, yet unneth ye shall
> Of our English tongue find any works
> Of cunning, that is regarded by clerks.
> The Greeks, the Romans, with many mo,
> In their mother tongue wrote warks excellent.
> Then if clerks in this realm would take pain so,
> Considering that our tongue is now sufficient
> ............................................
> They might, if they would, in our English tongue
> Write works of gravity sometime among. (p. 7)

The interlude commences with Nature Naturata, the primary virtue character, instructing Humanity, the mankind figure, about nature's function and the four elements. The virtuous Humanity is an eager student, who promises that

> ... his felicity shall be most of all
> To study and to search for causes natural. (p. 16)

With the help of Studious Desire, he begins his education. But despite his good intentions, he is tempted and he falls. Weary of studying, he deserts Studious Desire and befriends Sensual Appetite, a Vice. His life in sin is indicated conventionally by a visit to a tavern, where Humanity commits the sins of gluttony and lechery. Although he leaves Sensual Appetite for a short time because Studious Desire introduces him to Experience, with whom

> ... I would take a word or two...
> For to satisfy my desire (p. 37),

Humanity does not return to his studies or recognize, as yet, the dangers of uncontrolled sensuality. While the second half of the play is imperfect, what exists suggests the full morality development. Humanity accepts Sensuality as his master and takes Sensual Appetite and Ignorance as his companions. The last page of the text, however, indicates that Humanity is about to repent. Nature berates him for his folly. Humanity excuses himself, stating that he never meant to oppose Nature's wishes and that he followed Sensual Appetite 'for necessity' only (p. 50). Nature refuses to accept this explanation:

> Though it be for thee full necessary
> For thy comfort sometime to satisfy
> Thy sensual appetite,
> Yet it is not convenient for thee
> To put therein thy felicity. (p. 50)

It seems probable that Humanity perceives his error, repents his sins, and promises to live virtuously by continuing his search for the 'causes natural'.

*The Nature of the Four Elements* uses morality elements to illustrate man's need for knowledge of the natural world. As we know from the play, this knowledge is strongly tied to religious conceptions of nature. Its characters and the struggles of the mankind figure are determined by this purpose. Consequently, the interlude provides another example of the movement toward particularization which occurs in these Tudor moral interludes. The play, moreover, reflects the contemporary humanistic concern with man's earthly life, a concern which, in this moral interlude, as well as in many others, was combined with the concern for man's spiritual well-being.

*Wyt and Science* deals with the struggle to obtain knowledge. Personified Wyt, the hero, is a young scholar who loves and seeks to wed the Lady Science. The plot borrows several elements from the romance: by learning the tools of 'science', Wyt undergoes the training necessary to win his love; he must prove himself worthy of her favor; and before she accepts him, he must overcome Tediousness, the giant who guards Mount Parnassus. Despite these romance elements the play belongs, as we shall see, to the morality tradition.

In the first place, its characters function like the Virtues, the Vices, and the mankind figure found in the moralities. Science, for example, recalls Salvation, the object man wishes to achieve. Wyt, desiring her but weak enough to be tempted by Idleness, is much like a mankind figure. Reason, who forgives Wyt his faults and helps him to win Lady Science, is similar to the virtue figure Mercy. Idleness is clearly Sloth, developed in terms of education. In his attempt to destroy Wyt, Tediousness is a typical Vice and is specifically called a 'fiend' by Instruction.[10]

Second, as the following summary will make clear, the play employs the morality structure. Although the initial scene is imperfect, Reason's first speech indicates that Wyt, because he desires to wed Lady Science, begins in a state of virtue. The problem of correct vision is introduced immediately, for Reason gives Wyt a mirror

> ...wherein beholde yee
> Youre-selfe to youreselfe. (ll. 2–3)

Wyt's fall results from his willful decision to pursue material so difficult that even with the aid of Study and Diligence he cannot master it. He is soon overcome by this material and 'dies'. Fortunately, however, he is 'resurrected' by Honest Recreation, Comfort, Quickness, and Strength. But he does not return to a life of virtue. Refusing to follow the counsel of Reason, he falls into the 'lap of Idleness'. His vision is so marred that he prefers her to Honest Recreation and does not recognize, as Recreation warns him, that she "Goth abowte to dyceve you..." (l. 391). While Wyt is in a trancelike state, Idleness places the coat of Ignorance on him. Thus dressed, he appears before the Lady Science. Although he thinks himself to be what he was, she recognizes him for the fool he has become. After she has rejected him and with the help of Reason's glass, Wyt finally perceives himself as he now is. He almost gives way to despair:

> Alas! that lady [Science] I have now lost
> Whome all the world lovth and honoryth most. (ll. 780–81)

---

[10] John Redford, *The Play of Wyt and Science*, in *Specimens of the Pre-Shakespearean Drama*, I, l. 905. Other references to the play will be made in the body of the text.

In a monologue, he confesses his follies and shows that he is contrite. His penance takes the form of a beating by Shame. Wyt finally seeks out Reason and begs his forgiveness. The virtue figure not only forgives him but, moreover, promises the youth that, because he has amended his ways, he may yet win the Lady Science. With the aid of Instruction, Wyt woos her again. Regenerate, he overcomes the giant Tediousness, and soon weds the lady he loves.

Finally, the play reflects the didactic concern of the older morality. On one level, the interlude demonstrates clearly the vices a young scholar should avoid and the virtues he must embrace in order to obtain knowledge. On another level, however, as the play's language indicates, the interlude is concerned with the problem of man's spiritual salvation. Wyt's follies not only threaten his marriage to Lady Science but, in addition, his spiritual welfare. He is told, for example, that Idleness, 'The verye roote of all vyciousness' (p. 433) will bring him to a 'shamefull end'. (p. 435) And because of his crimes, Wyt's face becomes 'as black as the devyll'. (p. 447) Reason, furthermore, accuses him of having done deeds 'offendying both God and man'. (p. 448) Such language implies that the slothful student is a fool who endangers both his earthly welfare and his spiritual well-being. Only the industrious scholar is able to obtain the knowledge he desires and to live virtuously by eschewing the vices which tempt him. By his industry, then, he obtains earthly happiness by obtaining what he most loves, while, at the same time, he lives in the best possible way for one who wishes to work toward the salvation of his soul. *Wyt and Science*, therefore, provides an excellent example of how the Tudor moral interlude fuses the problems of man's spiritual salvation and earthly happiness and deals with them both in terms of a particular topic.[11]

---

[11] *Wyt and Science* achieved great popularity. There are two extant imitations, *The Marriage of Wit and Science* (c. 1569), edited by John S. Farmer ("The Tudor Facsimile Texts", [Vol. XLII]; London and Edinburgh, T. C. & E. C. Jack, 1909), and *A Contract of Marriage between Wit and Wisdom* (c. 1579), *(ibid.*, [Vol. XLIII]). The latter is closer to the morality than the former. In *Wit and Wisdom*, Wit is beguiled by Idleness, Wantonness, and Fancy, but he realizes his mistake and eventually marries Wisdom. The importance of parents in the controlling of a child's education is shown through Wit's parents, his father, Severity, and his mother, Indulgence. Like Redford's hero, Wit is beguiled by Idleness and must overcome the

*Impatient Poverty* (c. 1560) is based upon the assumption that man's earthly happiness and rightful prosperity depend upon his spiritual condition. Peace, the major virtue figure, argues that worldly prosperity comes to those who avoid the sin of envy and who live virtuously:

> The puissant Prince and Innocent most pure,
> Which humbly descended from the seat sempiternal,
> Illumine his beams of grace to every creature;
> To withstand the conflict of our enemies mortal;
> The devil, the world, and the flesh, these three in special,
> Which setteth division between the soul and the body;
> In like wise envy setteth debate between party and party.
> I speak for this cause: daily ye may see
> How that, by envy and malice, many be destroyed;
> Which, if they had lived in peace with patient humility,
> Riches and prosperity with them had been employed[12]

The action begins after this statement of didactic intention. Envy debates with Peace but loses the argument and, calling for a constable to arrest his opponent, leaves the stage. Impatient Poverty, the mankind figure, then appears. Wrathful and envious, he debates with Peace concerning man's justice and God's love. Hoping to turn him from evil, Peace offers Poverty worldly riches,

> If thou wilt forsake sensuality
> And be governed by reason, as I shall induce thee. (p. 318)

After he has been reminded of Christ's sacrifice and after he has realized

---

giant, Ircksomeness, before he can marry Wisdom. *The Marriage of Wit and Science* is less like a morality and more like a romance. The romance elements, particularly the courtship, are emphasized. At first Will tries to dissuade Wit from marrying; Experience convinces Lady Science that she should marry. There are, however, some morality elements drawn from Redford's play: Wit falls into Idleness; he is at first defeated by Tediousness; finally, he conquers the giant, and, of course, he wins the lady. But in general the morality elements are relatively slight. Werner Habicht discusses romance elements, in "The *Wit*-Interludes and the Form of Pre-Shakespearean 'Romantic Comedy'", *Renaissance Drama*, Vol. XIII (Evanston, Northwestern University Press, 1965, 73-88).

[12] *Impatient Poverty*, in *Recently Recovered "Lost" Tudor Plays*, p. 313. Other references to the play will be made in the body of the text.

> That poverty and misery that I my life in lead
> It is but only punishment for my misdeed (p. 32),

Poverty turns from sin and promises to be counselled by Peace. His financial problems evaporate, and he becomes Prosperity. Obviously, in this interlude, the virtuous man finds his rewards in both worlds.

Nevertheless, as the next scene demonstrates, earthly possessions are not accurate gauges of a man's virtue. Abundance, the covetous man, is introduced. Despite the urgings of Conscience, he refuses to turn from sin. Conscience begs him to think of Judgment Day and, in so doing, implies that covetousness will bring Abundance to spiritual damnation:

> ... plunged by ignorance,
> Regarding nothing of ghostly instruction,
> Setting more his mind on worldly substance
> Than on the everlasting life that is to come!
> God will strike when He list; ye know not how soon. (p. 326)

His concern for man's spiritual well-being makes Conscience an enemy which a Vice must eliminate if he is to ensnare mankind and keep him in a state of sin. Disguised as Charity, Envy seeks out Conscience and frightens him so much that he leaves England. With Conscience gone, Envy believes he is now free to bring strife into the country.

Still disguised, the Vice proceeds to tempt the mankind figure. Poverty does not befriend him, however, until Envy mentions the three hundred pounds he possesses. Then, ignoring the warnings of Peace and forgetting his promise to live virtuously, Poverty succumbs to covetousness and chooses Envy as his companion. His ruin is assured. He becomes a prodigal, guided by Misrule whom he believes is Mirth. His life in sin is limited to one scene. After having lost his wealth and, as a result, having been abandoned by his companions, Poverty finally sees that he has been blind to the natures of Envy and Misrule and to his own spiritual condition as well. Contrite, he confesses his crimes and appears before the Court to do open penance for theft. While there, he meets Peace, from whom he begs and receives forgiveness:

> Thou art well punished for thy trespass.
> By thine own sensual and undiscreet operation
> Hath brought thee to all this tribulation. (p. 346)

Once more in a state of virtue, the regenerate Poverty becomes, once more, Prosperity. And, consequently, in spite of Peace's warning that man's fortunes are transitory, the play teaches the members of the audience that the virtuous man can expect to be prosperous as well.

*Impatient Poverty* is unusually interesting because in no other moral interlude is the problem of man's spiritual welfare related so completely to his earthly well-being. In addition, the social criticism which Louis Wright finds in "...plays with morality features..." of the 1560's and 1570's[13] is evident here. The scene between Abundance and Conscience, for instance, attacks the vices of contemporary England. Abundance justifies his sinfulness as the way of the world:

> If falsehood, usury, and extortion should rout,
> Thousands in this realm should be put;
> The third part should not bide, by Saint Paul! (pp. 324-25)

And although Abundance, like Poverty, is summoned to Court, he is able to escape just punishment because he is rich enough to bribe the Sumner. Yet while such social criticism unquestionably exists in the play, its presence must not obscure the fact that the interlude's primary concerns are man's earthly happiness and spiritual welfare.

The title of *The Contention Between Liberality and Prodigality* (1601)[14] suggests a debate between these allegorical characters. But while the play does consider the question of the proper control of wealth, much of it deals with the life in sin and the regeneration of Prodigality, who functions as a mankind figure. Having wasted his money, Prodigality is arraigned because, with others, he "...didst felloniusly take from one Tenacity..." one thousand pounds of gold and silver sterling.[15] After he has been brought

---

[13] Louis B. Wright, "Social Aspects of Some Related Moralities", *Anglia* (1930) p. 110.

[14] According to Alfred Harbage, in *Annals of English Drama 975-1701*, revised by S. Schoenbaum (London, Methuen and Co., Ltd., 1964), the play possibly may be a revival of the lost *Prodigality*, 1567 (p. 80).

[15] *The Contention Between Liberality and Prodigality*, edited by W. W. Greg ("The Malone Society Reprints". 1913-A; Cambridge, Oxford University Press, 1913), ll. 1265-67. Other references to the play will be included in the body of the text.

to justice, he perceives that he has been living a life of sin. Contrite, he confesses his faults:

> I confess I haue runne a wanton wicked race,
> Which now hath brought me to this wofull wretched case.
> I am hearthly sorrie, and with teares doe lament
> My former lewd, and vile misgouernment. (ll. 1298-1301)

He seeks mercy and asks the Judge, "To be a mean for him, that meaneth to amend." (l. 1305) The Judge promises him that once he has done penance, Prodigality will be forgiven his crimes. The play ends with Prodigality regenerated and with money under the control of Liberality. This work adds no new knowledge to the present study. But it does provide late examples of what we find in earlier interludes: the application of morality elements to a specific problem and the concern of most interludes with man's earthly life.

Four moral interludes examine the sources of a healthy and prosperous commonwealth. Skelton's *Magnyfycence* (1515-1523), the earliest of these, demonstrates that the well-being of a state depends upon the virtue of its prince.

The first scene dramatizes the appropriate relationship between Wealthy Felicity, Liberty, and Measure, the three qualities necessary for the proper government of a realm. Though each is important, Measure must have dominion, for, as Felicity points out,

> ...without Measure, Pouerte and Nede
> Wyll crepe vpon vs, and vs to Myschefe lede.[16]

In the second scene, Magnyfycence, the mankind figure, is introduced. That he begins in a state of virtue is clear from his acceptance of Liberty, Felicity, and Measure as "Conuenyent persons for any prynce ryall" (l. 173), and by his recognition that, of the three, Measure must take precedence.

As a prince, Magnyfycence should be wiser than those he rules. But like all men he is capable of erroneous judgments. Although

---

[16] Robert Lee Ramsey (ed.), *Magnyfycence, a Moral Play by John Skelton* ("Early English Text Society", Extra Series, XCVIII, London, Kegan Paul, Trench, Trubner and Co., Limited, 1908), ll. 53-54. Other references to the play will be made in the body of the text.

at first he berates Largesse for his evil counsel, he does not perceive that Largesse is not what he appears, to be, that he is, in fact, the Vice Fancy. By appealing to Magnyfycence's desire to be a popular ruler, Fancy soon wins the confidence of the Prince and becomes a trusted counsellor. Once Fancy has been admitted to Magnyfycence's court, other Vices, such as Counterfeit Countenance, Cloaked Collusion, and Courtly Abusion, are welcomed too.

The Prince, then, has fallen from a life of virtue into a life of sin. The depth of his fall is reflected in his excessive pride:

> Fortune to her lawys can not abandune me;
> But I shall of Fortune rule the reyne.
> I fere nothynge Fortunes perplextye;
> All Honour to me must nedys stowpe and lene. (ll. 1459-62)

Surrounded by his evil counsellors, the proud Magnyfycence rejects Measure and accepts Folly in his place. As a result he brings Adversity, God's punishment for the followers of Fancy and Folly, to himself and to his kingdom.

Magnyfycence is, of course, capable of regeneration. Through Adversity, his spiritual vision begins to be corrected:

> Alasse that euer I magnyfycence was named!
> ... Alasse that I could not myslfe no better gyde! (ll. 1983, 1986)

Despair tempts the Prince to believe himself unworthy of mercy; he is about to commit suicide when Good Hope enters and takes the sword from him. With the aid of Good Hope, Magnyfycence's faith is restored, and he repents. This repentance is not developed fully but, instead, is suggested by Magnyfycence's statement:

> ...sore I repent me of my Wylfulnesse;
> I aske God Mercy of my Neglygesse. (ll. 2379-80)

That he is contrite is established by Good Hope, who tells Redress, Magnyfycence "... is sory for that he hath offendyd". (l. 2388) His confession is indicated not only by his admission of willfulness but, in addition, by his admission to Redress that he is "A wrechyd man, Syr, to my Maker vnkynde". (l. 2390) He does no penance. The play ends with the regenerate Magnyfycence, forgiven his sins and in a 'state of grace' (l. 2403), promising to live virtuously and to govern with liberality, moderation, and magnanimity.

*Magnyfycence* follows the morality structure closely, but there are, nevertheless, some variations. As in several interludes discussed above, the first steps of the morality structure, the introduction of the Vices, is omitted, and the repentance of the mankind figure is not developed in any detail. More interesting, however, is the fact that this interlude is the first to use the morality pattern specifically for a political purpose: to demonstrate that a healthy and prosperous state depends upon the moral condition of its ruler. The play is of importance, furthermore, because it elevates the social position of the mankind figure. Except in *Pride of Life*, which is a special case, the mankind figures in the moralities cannot be considered to be of noble rank. The hero of *Mankind* is described as a farmer. While the social positions of the others are not given, we do know that none is a ruler. At any rate, the mankind figures in these older moralities are meant to be generalized representations of typical Christian man and, consequently, would not be limited to any particular social station. The use of a prince for a mankind figure, therefore, is significant because it illustrates yet another method by which morality elements are adapted to the special concern of a Tudor moral interlude.

The first part of David Lindsay's *Ane Pleasant Satyre of the Thrie Estaitis* (c. 1540) is also concerned with the relationship between the moral condition of a ruler and the well-being of his state. Although Rex Humanitas, the mankind figure, wishes to be a virtuous man and a virtuous ruler, he falls into a life of sin because he fails to control his sensual desires. As he explains it,

> I throw Cupido, with his dart,
> Hes woundit me out-throw the hart;
> My spreit will fra my bodie part,
> Get I nocht my desyre.[17]

Blinded by lust, he takes as counsellors the Vices Flattery, Dissait, and Falset, whom he believes to be Sapience, Discretion, and Devotion. Because of his uncontrolled sensuality and his evil

---

[17] Sir David Lindsay, *Ane Satyre of the Thrie Estaitis*, Part I, in *The Poetical Works of Sir David Lindsay*, edited by David Laing (Edinburgh, William Paterson, 1879), II, ll. 373-76. Other references to the play will be made in the body of the text. According to Laing, the general character of Rex Humanitas has some resemblances to that of James the Fifth (p. 3).

cousellors, the king becomes an inadequate ruler who threatens the welfare of his state. For, as Verities points out to him, a good ruler offers a pattern of virtue for those he rules, since

> ... subjects do follow, day and nicht,
> Their governours in vertew, and in vyce (ll. 1057-58),

and, a king "...sould of gude exempils be the well". (1. 1066). Without struggling against the temptation to despair, and with the aid of Correction, Rex Humanitas rejects the Vices he had embraced. He places himself under the command of Correction, who restores Vertue, Good Counsel, and Chastity to him. The regenerate Rex Humanitas ends as a virtuous ruler, whose only concern is "How I sall keip my Realme in rest" (l. 1881). While *The Thrie Estaitis* offers no new insights into the Tudor moral interlude, it does, however, indicate the dramatic vitality of those found in other works, especially *Magnyfycence*.

That any commonwealth may, for a time, fall into adversity is shown in *Respublica* (1553), a unique but interesting variation of the morality pattern.[18] Respublica, who functions as a mankind figure, has been deceived by the Vices Avarice, Adulation, Insolence, and Oppression, who disguised themselves as Policy, Honesty, Authority, and Reformation. Why she should be blind to their natures is never known. But since she has embraced them, despite her love for her subjects, the commonwealth decays because she receives ill counsel. Respublica's life in sin is represented by the results of ill counsel upon the state. Her character, however, is never marred by her association with the Vices. As soon as she realizes that her counsellors are evil, and without any temptation to despair, Respublica turns from them and toward the Virtues Misericordia, Veritas, Justice, and Pax. The morality pattern is completed only by an extraordinary disregard for dramatic probability. The Vices are arraigned and brought to trial. And they now function as mankind figures, repenting their sins, begging for mercy, and, finally, obtaining forgiveness for their crimes against the state. At the end of the play, the regenerate Vices have become the Virtues they had pretended to be. Wrong, therefore, is corrected by time, and truth and right reign again. *Respublica* clearly employs

[18] *Respublica*, in Farmer's *Recently Recovered "Lost" Tudor Plays*, pp. 177-272.

the morality pattern, but it does so with extraordinary freedom in order to celebrate the ascension in 1553 of 'Bloody' Mary to the throne of England.

*Wealth and Health* (c. 1557), the last of the Tudor interludes to be discussed which is concerned with the welfare of a state, provides another example of the way in which the mankind figure has been adapted to the particular needs of the play. In this work, the characters who function as mankind figures are the personifications of the qualities necessary for every realm: Health, Wealth, and Liberty.

As their promise to Remedy that they will "eschew ill and shrewd company"[19] illustrates, when the play opens, the three are in a state of virtue. Deceived by Ill-Will, Shrewd Wit, and Hance, however, they soon fall into a life of sin. Eventually, they realize that they have been tainted by their association with these Vices, and they seek the aid of Remedy, whose purpose is to maintain them in a nation. Although none struggles with despair, all three repent. Diseased Health is the first. Realizing that he has been blind: "Wit and Will hath deceived me: in them I put my trust" (p. 302), with the aid of Remedy, he captures the Vices and sends them to prison. Wealth's contrition and confession represent those of the others as well:

> In the hope of God we ask you forgiveness, all three;
> We ought to be ashamed to look you in the face.
> By our folly and negligence we have done so unwisely;
> We were foully deceived; we put us to your grace. (p. 306)

None does penance. Warning them to learn from experience to serve and love God, Remedy forgives them all: "I shall restore ye again as well as ever ye were." (p. 308) *Wealth and Health* demonstrates once again that virtue is the source of a commonwealth's well-being and prosperity.

Although the differences between the older morality plays and the Tudor moral interludes considered here are relatively few, they are, nevertheless, extremely important. In the older morality, there is

---

[19] *An Interlude of Wealth and Health*, in *Recently Recovered "Lost" Tudor Plays*, p. 295. Other references to the play will be included in the body of the text.

one didactic intention: to show man that he must eschew vice, repent his sins, and embrace virtue if he is to win spiritual salvation. In the Tudor moral interlude, on the other hand, there is a two — fold didactic intention: to teach man how to achieve not only his spiritual salvation but his earthly happiness as well. Both ends, however, are achieved by the same means. A man fulfills his social responsibilities only if he eschews vice and lives virtuously; by so doing he works toward the salvation of his soul. *Impatient Poverty* provides an excellent illustration. When Poverty is envious or prodigal, he threatens his spiritual welfare because he succumbs to sins which, at the same time, bring him to financial ruin. Yet when he follows the counsels of Peace and promises to live as a virtuous Christian should, he improves his spiritual condition as he restores his earthly prosperity. In these Tudor moral interludes, therefore, the problems of man's spiritual and earthly well-being are fused.

The political interludes enlarge the didactic intention of the morality even further by demonstrating that the welfare of a state depends upon a virtuous ruler. For when a ruler ignores his Christian duties, he not only threatens his own spiritual well-being and earthly happiness but those of his subjects as well. He can bring either adversity or prosperity to his state; and since he is their model, his subjects follow him in virtue or in vice.

The action of the interlude reflects this didactic concern with man's earthly existence. On one level, it deals with the same conflict found in the morality play, that between the Vices and the Virtues for possession of mankind's soul. On another level, however, it deals with the conflict between those trying to lead mankind to behaviour which is socially condemned and those trying to turn him toward behaviour which is socially approved. *Lusty Juventus* will illustrate. Hypocrisy and Wicked Fellowship tempt Juventus to lead a life of sin which threatens his spiritual salvation and which would bring about his social condemnation, since by following these Vices the youth avoids his social responsibilities.

Unlike the older moralities and probably as a result of the concern with man's earthly existence, most of these Tudor moral interludes are limited to a particular subject and attempt to resolve some contemporary problem. *Lusty Juventus*, for example, argues that only the 'New Gospel' offers religious truth and that Catholicism is the way of the Devil. *The Nature of the Four Elements* teaches man much about the natural world and why such knowledge is necessary for his welfare. The political interludes demonstrate the need for a ruler to be virtuous and to choose his counsellors wisely.

This limitation of subject matter leads to the particularization of action and character, for both are developed in light of the specific problem considered. In *Wyt and Science*, for instance, the conflict is between those seeking to turn Wyt into Ignorance and those seeking to wed him to the Lady Science. In *Lusty Juventus* it is between those seeking to corrupt England's youth through Catholicism or sensual living and those wishing to save him through the 'New Gospel'.

While only the three basic morality characters – the Virtues, the Vices, and the mankind figure – are present in these Tudor moral interludes, they, too, reflect the particular concerns of the individual plays. With reference again to *Wyt and Science*, Idleness and Tediousness, like Study and Diligence, are, respectively, the Vices and the Virtues most appropriate for a work limited to the problem of the education of a youth. The mankind figure undergoes great change, and in most interludes he is no longer abstract humanity. He becomes, instead, a type, be it mankind the youth, the student, or the prince.

The tendency to particularize – to make concrete what has been abstract – is the tendency to turn dramatic allegory into realistic drama. The ultimate result is the separation of action and plot, that is, the separation between the essential conflict which a play dramatizes and the unique handling of the story, through which the action is made concrete. In the older morality plays, the differences between action and plot are minor. In these Tudor moral interludes, however, a separation begins to occur. The action deals with the conflict between the Vices and the Virtues for control of mankind's soul and between the forces of evil and the forces of good for control of his earthly behavior. But this action is placed within a specific context and develops a specific problem. *Wyt and Science* will illustrate. The action concerns the conflict between the Vices and the Virtues for the soul and mind of the hero. The plot develops this action by the trials Wyt undergoes and the battles he wages to woo and win the Lady Science. While the separation between action and plot is not fully realized in these interludes, it does suggest what occurs in the morality-patterned comedy, the complete separation of action and plot. In *How a Man May Chuse*, for example, the action deals with the conflict between the virtue and the vice figures for Arthur's soul and his social behaviour. The plot particularizes this action by placing it in contemporary London and developing it through Arthur's intended crime, his second marriage, and his trial. In these Tudor moral interludes, then, lies the potential for the morality-patterned comedies.

The full structure of the older moralities consists of seven steps: the introduction of the Vices, the introduction of Mankind in a state of virtue, his temptation and fall, his life in sin, the temptation for him to despair, his repentance, and his forgiveness. While these Tudor moral interludes generally follow this same structure, a few changes occur. First, the introduction of the Vices seldom begins the interlude. *Nature*, for example, begins with a lesson to Mankind concerning her role. Second, man's life in sin is developed more fully in these interludes than it is in the older moralities. In *Hyckescorner* and *Mundus et Infans*, to cite only two works, it takes up over half the play. Third, as in the political interludes, the temptation to despair may be omitted. Fourth, mankind's repentance may not be as fully developed as it is in the early moralities. That of *Magnyfycence*, for example, is clearly limited. These changes increase the flexibility of the morality pattern, making it adaptable to the particular needs of a particular play. At the same time, they illustrate the durability of the overall morality structure; for excluding the introduction of the Vices (the least important step for the development of the action) and occasionally the temptation to despair, the structural sequence remains the same despite alterations occurring within particular sections.

Consequently, these Tudor interludes differ from the older moralities in three ways. They expand the didactic intention to include the problem of man's earthly well-being. They particularize the morality action, structure, and characters by limiting the play to a specific and, usually, contemporary problem. And they vary the morality structure somewhat by omitting, at times, the introduction of the Vices or the temptation to despair and by dealing with one step in great detail while another is merely sketched. These changes are significant because they indicate changes which occur in the morality-patterned comedies.

One problem remains. Why would those Tudor moral interludes which employ the morality pattern lead to comedy? The answer is readily apparent. The full development of the morality structure requires that the Virtues vanquish the Vices and that the mankind figure be forgiven his sins. This merciful conclusion provides the happy ending necessary for comedy. The interludes, furthermore, follow a movement typical of comedy: either they begin in trouble, or, in those plays where the mankind figure begins in a state of virtue, they soon come to it, and they always end in peace. We can say, therefore, that the movement of the morality structure is inherently comic and, consequently, that any fully-developed morality play or moral interlude is associated with the comic genre.

IV

THE MORALITY-PATTERNED COMEDY

The seventeen plays identified at the beginning of this study as morality-patterned comedies are united by the following features. Their central characters may be considered mankind figures, whose fall and regeneration are the main concern of the play. If the mankind figure begins in a state of virtue, his temptation and fall are part of the dramatic structure. All deal with the mankind figure's life in sin and his repentance. They end with him forgiven his crimes and restored to his appropriate position. These comedies, therefore, employ the pattern isolated in the older moralities.

They differ from the older moralities, however, in three ways. First, they reflect the changes in the morality pattern which developed in the Tudor moral interludes. As in these interludes, the problem of man's spiritual welfare is fused with the problem of his earthly well-being. And the concern for the mankind figure's welfare may be broadened to a concern with the welfare of an entire society. In addition, the structure of the morality pattern has become looser. Except in one comedy, the introduction of the vice figures, the first step in a morality opening with the mankind figure in a state of virtue, is omitted. The section dealing with the mankind figure's life in sin may be extended, while that dealing with his repentance may be contracted. Second, unlike the older moralities and the Tudor moral interludes, these works cannot be considered allegorical, although, occasionally, an allegorical figure may be used. Through the plot, the action has become particularized so that dramatized allegory is replaced by realistic drama, that is, drama presenting possible occurrences in the life of a man who has his own unique history. Though, on one level, the central character is a representative mankind figure, he is, on another level and at the same time, a particular individual living in a particular time and place. Third, as the forthcoming analyses will demonstrate, these plays are comedies meant to amuse their audience as well as to instruct them.

Despite the fact that the morality-patterned comedies are united by the features outlined above, not all of them utilize all the morality elements. As we have seen in the examination of the older moralities and the Tudor moral interludes, the morality pattern is exactly that – a pattern, not a prescription. Consequently, in order to establish the characteristics of the morality-patterned comedy and to indicate the variations within this group, all plays belonging to the category will be discussed below except *How a Man May Chuse*, which was analyzed earlier. To clarify the extent to which the individual plays exhibit morality elements, the discussion will begin with the core and proceed according to the number of variations occurring within each play. This examination prepares the way for a more general discussion of the morality-patterned comedy, involving the identifying features of the category, the ways in which it is similar to and different from the older morality plays, and, finally, why the plays of which it is composed can be considered comic.

The five plays making up the core of morality-patterned comedies were written within four years of one another. The earliest is *How a Man May Chuse* (c. 1601–1602); the latest, *Eastward Ho* (1605). *The Faire Maide of Bristow* and *The Dutch Curtezan* open with the mankind figure in a state of virtue. Both reflect the evolution examined in the Tudor interludes and omit the introduction of the Vices, the first step in the fully developed older moralities. *How a Man May Chuse*, The First Part of *The Honest Whore*, and *Eastward Ho* open with the mankind figure in the midst of his life in sin. In all but *The Honest Whore*, the mankind figure is a young man; in that play, as the title suggests, the mankind figure is a courtesan. None is of noble rank. Except for *Eastward Ho*, the predominant sin to which the mankind figure succumbs is lust; in *Eastward Ho*, it is prodigality.

*How a Man May Chuse* (c. 1601–1602), possibly written by Thomas Heywood, has already been examined. The four plays remaining to be discussed will be taken up in chronological order: *The Faire Maide* (1603–1604); *The Dutch Curtezan* (1603–1604) by John Marston; Part I of *The Honest Whore* (1604) by Thomas Dekker and Thomas Middleton; and, finally, *Eastward Ho* (1605) by Ben Jonson, George Chapman, and John Marston.

Like *How a Man May Chuse* and *The Dutch Curtezan*, the main plot of *The Faire Maide of Bristow* (1603–1604) illustrates the difference between love and lust.¹ It does so in two ways: as in *How a Man May Chuse*, a comparison is made between a courtesan and wife; and as in *The Dutch Curtezan*, a friend reveals to the courtesan's lover the folly of his passion.

The three central characters are developed in terms of the types found in the older morality play. Florence, the courtesan, functions throughout the play as the major vice figure. She tempts Vallenger to desert his wife, and in order to obtain his wealth, she seeks to have him murder both his wife and her lover so that they may wed. Finally, her treatment of Vallenger once he becomes penniless brings him close to despair and to the point of suicide. Annabell, Vallenger's wife, is the major virtue figure. Her love, of course, has the blessing of heaven. Unlike her elders, who demand justice for Valenger's crimes, Annabell offers him love and mercy. Indeed, her love for her husband is so great that she is even willing to sacrifice her life in order to save his. As do the mercy figures in the moralities, she hears Vallenger's confession, accepts his statement of repentance, and forgives him. Vallenger, as the plot summary will demonstrate, is a typical mankind figure.

At the beginning of the play, he falls in love with Annabell and marries her, although by so doing he betrays his friend, Challenger, who introduced the fair maid to him. On his wedding day, he sees the courtesan Florence, and, tempted by her beauty, he abandons his wife. Blinded by lust, he proves himself incapable of distinguishing between the worth of a wife and the worthlessness of a courtesan. Annabell, he now finds, is 'as trash and weedes' when compared with Florence, 'the violet'.² Bewitched, he agrees to murder Sentlo, Florence's lover, and his own wife so that he may be free to marry the courtesan. His crimes are never achieved, however, because his family is informed of them. He is, nevertheless, accused of murder. Hoping to replace her lover Sentlo with the wealthier Vallenger, Florence bribes her servant (who is Harbart,

---

¹ See Chapter I, page 17, note 6, for a statement regarding the debt of this play to *How a Man May Chuse* and *The Dutch Curtezan*.

² *The Faire Maide of Bristow*, edited by Arthur Hobson Quinn ("Publications of the University of Pennsylvania Series in Philology and Literature", Vol. VIII, No. 1; Philadelphia, Ginn and Co., 1902) ll. 319–20. Other references to the play will be made in the body of the text.

Sentlo's virtuous friend, in disguise) to poison him. When Vallenger is disinherited, she succeeds in having him blamed for the purported crime. After Florence has thus betrayed him, Vallenger is on the verge of suicide, but he is arrested before he can kill himself. Though innocent, he confesses to the murder of Sentlo as well as to the intended murder of his wife so that through death he can "rid my life of that foule spot". (l. 886) That he is acting out of despair is made clear by Annabell:

> Alas, poore soule, how griefe and his disgrace,
> Doth make him desperate. (ll. 887-88)

Once he has been sentenced to death, Vallenger repents. Contrite, he confesses his sins and begs forgiveness from those he has wronged:

> I do imbrace the law, as pleased to die,
> Father forgiue the follies of my unfained repentance
> Umphreuill, let me beare to heauen
> Upon the wings of my unfained repentance
> My sorrow heere indented in my tears,
> And thou indued wonder of thy sexe,
> Forgiue the wrongs that I haue done to thee,
> That I may goe with peace unto my death. (ll. 977-84)

The supposedly dead Sentlo does not come forward, however, until Vallenger's regeneration has been tested. The King decides that Vallenger can be released from execution if, since human justice requires that a death pay for a death, someone will die in his stead. Both Annabell and Challenger offer to do so. The King chooses Annabell upon the condition that her husband execute her. Vallenger refuses, and a few moments later Sentlo reveals himself. The repentant husband, consequently, is saved from death because no murder has been committed.

Having shown himself virtuous, Vallenger is restored to his appropriate place as a beloved son and as the beloved husband of a virtuous wife. Perhaps to insure that his wife may have no doubts about his amendment, he repents a second time, begging Annabell to

> Forget in me what I haue done amisse,
> And seale my pardon with one balmy kisse
> My soule repents her lewd impyetie. (ll. 1194-96)

She forgives him once more and even declares that she finds him dearer to her than he was at first; for now that Vallenger has knowledge of sin, she is certain he will prove virtuous. At the very end of the play, Florence becomes so touched by the willingness of Annabell and Challenger to die for the erring husband that, as the King's concluding speech informs us, possibly, "She sorrowes somthing for her follies past." (l. 1218) Hoping that she may repent, the King sends her to convent.

Through the experiences of Vallenger, *A Faire Maide* demonstrates vividly the threat vice poses for man's earthly happiness and his spiritual well-being. It serves, therefore, as

> ...a glasse for such as liues by lust,
> See what tis to be honest, what tis to be iust. (ll. 1176-77)

The main plot of John Marston's *The Dutch Curtezan* (1603-1604)[3] is also concerned with the difference between love and lust. Although the Prologue states that Marston's purpose is "...not to instruct, but to delight",[4] the play has a clear didactic function. For as the *Fabule argumentum* tells us, it illustrates, "The difference betwixt the love of a Curtezan, & a wife..." (p. 69).

Malheureux, the mankind figure, begins in a state of virtue; but, as the first scene shows, this virtue reflects his naiveté, not his ability to withstand temptation. Although Frevill's comments about lust are obviously sarcastic, Malheureux believes him to be serious. Whereas Frevill's description of Francischina, the Dutch courtesan, demonstrates that he realizes the attractiveness and so the danger of lust, Malheureux's remark shows that he does not. To him, a courtesan must be ugly because she is "...the most odious spectacle the earth can present, ...an immodest vulgar woman". (p. 75) He agrees to meet Francischina only in

---

[3] Robert K. Presson ("Marston's *Dutch Courtizan*: The Study of an Attitude in Adaptation", *The Journal of English and Germanic Philology*, LV (July, 1955), 406-13) comes to the conclusion that the play has morality elements. But he does not consider Frevill to be a virtue figure, simply one of the comrades of the mankind figure, and he emphasizes more than I do the role of Beatrice in the world view of virtue and vice.

[4] John Marston, *The Dutch Curtezan*, in *The Plays of John Marston*, edited by H. Harvey Wood (London and Edinburgh, Oliver and Boyd, 1938), II, 69. Other references to the play will be made in the body of the text.

order "...to make her loath the shame shee's in. The sight of vice augments the hate of sinne." (p. 75)

When he meets her, however, Malheureux falls from virtue. Blinded by Francischina's beauty, he refuses to perceive her spiritual condition:

> I never saw a sweet face vitious,
> It might be proud, inconstant, wanton, nice,
> But never tainted with unnaturall vice. (p. 79)

To justify his lust, which he had previously described as

> ...the strongest argument that speakes
> Against the soules eternite... (p. 73).

he decides it is a necessary part of love. And so that he can enjoy the courtesan, he is willing, if need be, to murder Frevill and to damn himself. Francischina tells him he must kill Frevill, her former lover, before she will become his mistress. Malheureux asks Frevill to help him dupe Francischina by pretending that they have fought and that Malhuereux has slain him.

Once she believes Frevill to be dead, Francischina betrays Malheureux. He is brought to trial and, since Frevill cannot be located, is sentenced to death. Francischina's betrayal succeeds in making Malheureux see the courtesan for the 'wicked Devill' (p. 126) she is. Condemned to die for a crime of which he is innocent, Malheureux almost gives way to despair, for he believes that while

> No kind of death is shamefull but the cause
> Which I do know is none, ...yet my lust
> Hath made the one (although not cause) most just. (p. 132)

He does not, however, despair. He requests a reprieve until Frevill may be found, but it is denied. Having made his 'endless Peace' (p. 133) and so demonstrating his faith in divine mercy, the contrite Malheureux confesses his sin and, thus, proves that he is regenerate:

> Oh how I lothe
> The very memory of that I adorde. (p. 133)

His sentence and the public airing of his sins can be considered as a form of penance, for through them Malheureux pays dearly for what he has done. As soon as Malheureux repents, the 'murdered' Frevill appears to save his life. Malheureux's return to virtue is clear from his remark to Frevill that "I am now worthie yours". (p. 134) Through his trials, he has learned all too well, "He that lust rules cannot be vertuous." (p. 134)

Malheureux, Francischina, and Frevill represent the three character types found in the morality. As the above discussion illustrates, Malheureux is a typical mankind figure. Francischina operates as a Vice. The intensity of her hatred and her desire for revenge upon Frevill, Beatrice (Frevill's fiancée), and Malheureux make her seem almost inhuman. Consequently, as Frevill describes her, she is

> ...beyond all
> Measure of Grace damnd immediatlie. (p. 127)

Certainly, this 'faire Devil' (p. 133) functions as a Vice in her attempt to control the behaviour of Malheureux. For if she had succeeded in tempting him to murder Frevill, she might well have brought him to spiritual damnation. Contrasted with her is Frevill, who functions as a virtue figure. Since Beatrice, his fiancée, has all the spiritual qualities which Francischina lacks, his love for her helps to identify him with the forces of good. Though he introduces Malheureux to the courtesan, once he realizes that his friend has been bewitched, he tries to dissuade him from a life of sin, first by means of reason and then by manipulation. As he assures the audience, he pretends to help Malheureux enjoy Francischina only to bring about his repentance:

> Ile be thy friend,
> But not thy Vices; and with greatest sence
> Ill force thee feele thy errors, to the worst. (p. 115)

We may say, then, that Frevill saves Malheureux from potential damnation as he saves him from death. Through him, Malheureux learns that vice can be attractive and that, for his earthly and spiritual welfare, man must withstand its temptations.

In the main plot of *The Dutch Curtezan*, the problem of man's spiritual well-being is made more explicit than it is in many morality-patterned comedies. The language of the play continually points up the conflict between good and evil involved in Malheureux's pursuit of Francischina. And as the lines cited in this discussion demonstrate, the threat which lust poses for man's spiritual salvation is the central concern of the play. In order to illustrate that lust is not only dangerous but ultimately less satisfying than love, the honorable love of Frevill for Beatrice is contrasted with the lust of Malheureux for Francischina. Frevill has experienced the pleasures which lust offers man. He knows that chaste love for a virtuous woman, not lust for a courtesan, is the source of true earthly joy:

> Heaven to have such a wife
> Is happiness to breed pale envy in the saintes. (p. 120)

From *The Dutch Curtezan*, therefore, the members of the audience learn that eschewing vice, repenting one's sins, and embracing virtue is the best means of achieving not only one's spiritual salvation but one's earthly happiness as well.

Because of its main plot, the First Part of *The Honest Whore* (1604), by Thomas Dekker and Thomas Middleton, belongs with those morality-patterned comedies concerned with the sin of lust. As in the two discussed above, a courtesan is a major character. Here, though, she becomes the mankind figure, and the play deals with her regeneration.

The work opens with Bellafront in the midst of her life in sin, but her repentance occurs early. Having fallen in love with Hippolito, she tries to seduce him. But he is repelled by her sinfulness and rejects her avowals of love. In order to dissuade her, he describes the evils of her profession so vividly that Bellafront realizes her spiritual corruption:

> You haue no soule,
> That makes you wey so light: heauens treasure bought it,
> And halfe a crowne hath sold it: for your body,
> Its like the common shoare, that still receiues
> All the townes filth.[5]

---

[5] Thomas Dekker and Thomas Middleton, *The Honest Whore*, Part I, in *The Dramatic Works of Thomas Dekker*, edited by Fredson Bowers, II (Cambridge: The University Press, 1955), II, i, 322-26. Other references to the play will be made in the body of the text. The Second Part, which includes fewer morality elements, will be discussed later.

Through Hippolito, therefore, Bellafront's spiritual vision is corrected, and, consequently, her regeneration begins. She weeps for her sins and confesses her foulness. Overcome with shame, she attempts suicide, but is saved by Hippolito, who takes the dagger from her. Bellafront decides, then, to turn honest in order to win Hippolito's love.

The motive for her regeneration differs from that of other mankind figures. The latter, once they perceive the evil reality of sin, turn from it because they actively desire to follow virtue. Bellafront's repentance, on the other hand, is based upon her love for Hippolito, and she wishes to become virtuous so that he will find her worthy. Yet even when he rejects her again, she does not forsake a life of virtue. For her love of Hippolito, whom she loves for his virtues (see II, i, 448-51), has led her, in the end, to love not only him but the ideal of virtue itself.

The trials and humiliation which Bellafront undergoes because she has turned honest serve as a form of penance. Having proved herself honest, she is rewarded, for Matheo, her first lover, is required by the Duke to marry her as appropriate recompense for the wrong he did her.

Part I employs the morality character types. Bellafront, of course, is the mankind figure, immersed in sin but capable of regeneration. By providing the motivation and being a means of Bellafront's regeneration, Hippolito functions as a virtue figure. The Vices fall into two groups. First, there are Bellafront's companions in sin, particularly Roger, her servant, and Mistress Fingerlock, a bawd. Second, Matheo, her first lover and later her husband, functions as a vice figure throughout most of the play. It was he who first tempted Bellafront to fall, and it is he who encouraged her sinfulness.

*Eastward Ho* (1605) by Jonson, Chapman, and Marston is unique among the morality-patterned comedies because it is the only one to parody the very morality elements it employs.[6] The play opens with the apprentice Quicksilver in the midst of his life in sin. His sinfulness is indicated particularly by his prodigality and by his friendship with Security, a usurer. After an ill-fated Virginian

[6] Miss Bradbrook sees the play as a parody of the "Old Prodigal Plays" but does not see any morality elements *(The Growth and Structure of Elizabethan Comedy,* London, Chatto and Windus, 1955, p. 47).

venture, Quicksilver is charged by Touchstone, his master, with suspicion of felony. Touchstone forces the apprentice to see the folly of his blindness to vice by summarizing the results of his sins:

> ...you see the issue of your Sloth. Of Sloth commeth Pleasure, of Pleasure commeth Riot, of Ryot comes Whoring, of Whoring comes Spending, of Spending comes Want, of Want comes Theft, of Theft comes Hanging; and there is my Quickesiluer fixt.[7]

Quicksilver is overcome with shame. After hearing the charge, he almost despairs of escaping execution: "O me, what an infortunate thing am I!" (IV, ii, 313) But he learns to accept his fate with Christian patience, deciding that if God so disposes, he will be hanged. He does contrive, nevertheless, to have Touchstone hear his song of repentance.

This song is a parody of the traditional steps of repentance. To the tune of "I wail in woe, I plunge in pain", Quicksilver confesses his sins and is properly contrite:

> Yet, woe is me, I would not learne,
> I saw, alas, but could not discerne.
> I cast my Coat and Cap away,
> I went in silkes, and sattens gay,
> False Mettall of good manners, I
> Did dayly coine unlawfully.
> . . . . . . . . . . . . . . . . .
> Yet I desire this grace to winne,
> That I may cut off the Horse-head of Sin,
> And leaue his body in the dust
> Of sinnes high way and bogges of Lust,
> Wherby I may take Vertues purse,
> And liue with her for better, for worse. (V, v, 57-62; 98-103)

He begs for mercy and promises to lead a godly life. As a result, he obtains Touchstone's forgiveness, reverses his master's opinion of him, and is released from prison when Touchstone drops the felony charges. The regenerate Quicksilver is free to do the penance

---

[7] Ben Jonson, George Chapman, and John Marston, *Eastward Ho*, in *Ben Jonson*, edited by C. H. Herford and Percy Simpson, IV (Oxford, The Clarendon Press, 1932), IV, ii, 324-27. Other references to the play will be made in the body of the text.

he desires, to "...goe home, through the streetes, in these, as a Spectale, or rather an Example, to the Children of Cheapeside". (V, v, 201-3) Touchstone ends the play with an address to the audience which sums up the moral significance of the action. Obviously, it, too, is a parody:

> ...Now London, looke about,
> And in this morrall, see thy Glasse runne out:
> Behold the carefull Father, thrifty Sonne;
> The solemne deeds, which each of us haue done;
> The Vsurer punisht, and from Fall so steepe
> The Prodigall child reclaimd, and the lost Sheepe. (V, v, 205-10)

Three characters function as do the character types found in the morality play. Security, the usurer, functions as a vice figure, for he tempts Quicksilver to fall deeper and deeper into a life of sin by receiving the stolen goods Quicksilver brings him, by giving lodging to his whores, and by welcoming the evil companions he brings to his house. Touchstone, on the other hand, functions as a virtue figure, for he warns Quicksilver to change his ways, hears the apprentice's repentance, and forgives him his crimes, as he shows by dropping the charges of felony. Quicksilver functions as a typical mankind figure who is sinful but capable of regeneration. He is contrasted with Golding, Touchstone's second apprentice, who represents the thrifty and wise citizen. While Quicksilver's fortunes decline, Golding's rise. Because of his virtue, the latter makes an excellent match with his master's daughter and rises to the honored positions of alderman and deputy. This contrast is meant, of course, to dramatize the contrast between the fruits of vice and the rewards of virtue. It does not, however, alter Quicksilver's role as the type of mankind figure we are examining in this study.

To conclude, even so limited a discussion as this one indicates that much of the amusement in *Eastward Ho* depends upon a parody of the morality elements it contains. This parody is especially valuable to the present study; for it suggests that an Elizabethan audience must have been familiar with the morality pattern. Otherwise, it seems unlikely that Jonson, Chapman, and Marston would have depended so heavily upon it for comic effects.

Each of the remaining twelve plays considered morality-patterned comedies lack or vary at least one of the formal elements isolated in the older moralities. Those most often missing are the temptation to despair and penance, both of which are omitted in some of the Tudor interludes examined. As the following discussions demonstrate, although the didactic intention found in the older moralities exists as well in these comedies, it is sometimes implicit rather than explicit. Of the plays to be studied, three are concerned with the welfare of a state; the others are concerned with the private affairs of the mankind figure. Only three plays begin with him in a state of virtue; the rest open with him in the midst of a life in sin.

Because this study attempts to illustrate the degree to which individual plays utilize the morality pattern, the discussion is organized according to groups based upon the number of elements omitted or varied. Since there is no particular pattern to these variations, the discussions within groups is chronological.

Each of the four plays to be taken up next lacks one element: the vice is a minor character in *A Looking Glasse for London and England* (1587-1591), by Robert Greene and Thomas Lodge; *All's Well That Ends Well* (c. 1601-c. 1604), by William Shakespeare, omits the temptation to despair; penance is omitted in *Misogonus* (c. 1560-1577), possibly by Laurence Johnson, Thomas Richards, or Anthony Rudd, and *If This Be Not a Good Play, the Devils' In It* (1611-1612), by Thomas Dekker. *A Looking Glasse* and *If This Be Not a Good Play* (like *Histrio-mastix* which will be discussed later) are political comedies dealing with the welfare of a state. As one might expect, in both plays, the mankind figures are kings. Lust is the predominant sin to which Bertram, the mankind figure in *All's Well*, succumbs, while prodigality is that to which Misogonus yields. Bertram is a count; Misogonus is a commoner.

Based upon the Old Testament account of Ninevah in the "Book of Jonah", *A Looking Glasse for London and England* (c. 1587-1591), by Robert Greene and Thomas Lodge, is the earliest of the three morality-patterned comedies concerned with the welfare of a state. Its purpose is to warn the members of the London audience that their sins endanger the well-being of their nation. Unless they turn from evil, repent, and live virtuously, God may destroy England as he threatened to destroy Ninevah:

> London, awake, for feare the Lord do frowne;
> I set a looking glasse before thine eyes,
> O turne, O turne, with weeping to the Lord,

And thinke the praiers and vertues of thy Queene
Defers the plague which otherwise would fall.
Repent, O London...[8]

The play opens with the numerous mankind figures, representing a cross-section of Ninevah's inhabitants, immersed in their lives in sin. Since it is meant to reflect the moral condition of contemporary England, this segment of the morality structure receives extended treatment. The sins presented are certainly horrendous: Rasni, the King of Ninevah, attempts to marry his sister and to seduce Aluida, the Queen of Paphagonia. Aluida, in turn, seduces the King of Cilicia and murders her husband. And by means of a legal trick, a usurer cheats his debtors and obtains their lands and wealth. Although, as these examples might lead us to believe, the mankind figures seem almost totally depraved, they are, nevertheless, capable of regeneration, once Jonah has warned them of God's anger and informed them of His intention to destroy the town. Finally aware of their sins and overcome with shame, they struggle with the temptation to despair. Rasni, for instance, states: "My soule is burned in the hell of thoughts" (V, i, 1909); Aludia asks,

...how dare we looke on heavenly light,
That haue dispisde the maker of the same?
How may we hope for mercie from aboue,
That still dispise the warnings from above? (V, i, 1927-30)

She and Rasni soon succeed in overcoming the temptation to despair, and with their faith restored, both beg for mercy. The temptation to despair is dramatized most fully by the usurer, who appears "with a halter in one hand, a dagger in the other". An Evil Angel encourages him to commit suicide, but he resists the temptation to do so because a voice

...bids me staie, and tels me that the Lord
Is mercifull to those that do repent. (V, ii, 1962-63)

---

[8] Robert Greene and Thomas Lodge, *A Looking Glasse for London and England*, in *The Plays & Poems of Robert Greene*, edited by J. Churton Collins, I (Oxford, The Clarendon Press, 1905), V, v, 2276-81. Other references to the play will be made in the body of the text.

The confession of all mankind figures consists of their acknowledgment of sin. Contrition and penance are indicated by means of prayers, the wearing of sackcloth, and fasting, traditional methods of seeking grace and those mentioned specifically in the Biblical account. Once the citizens have turned from evil, God pities them and sends Jonah to Ninevah to "...bring glad tydings of recouered grace". (V, iii, 2119) Through divine mercy, therefore, the lives and the souls of the citizens of Ninevah are saved. And, thus, the play teaches the Englishman that he, too, can save himself and his country from God's wrath.

The morality pattern is suited perfectly to the subject matter of *A Looking Glasse*. It provides Greene and Lodge with convenient tools for turning a short Biblical narrative into a full-scale drama. While the play uses most morality elements, it does vary them in terms of its concern with the moral condition of contemporary England. The section dealing with mankind's life in sin has been expanded and that dealing with his repentance has been contracted. Because it deals with the welfare of an entire nation, numerous mankind figures from all social ranks are employed, although Rasni, the King of Ninevah, is the central one. As are the kings in the political interludes, he is ultimately responsible for the moral condition of his subjects:

> My life hath bene a loadstarre vnto them,
> To guide them in the laborinth of blame. (V, ii, 1999-2000)

The virtue characters are limited to the prophets, Jonah and "Ossea". Unlike most moralities and moral interludes, and except for the Evil Angel, who appears once and then only briefly, the play is devoid of vice figures. Instead, the vices which the mankind figures have embraced are illustrated by their behaviour. Rasni's lust, for example, is clear from his seduction of Aluida, and the usurer's covetousness is obvious from his deception of two debtors. This method of presenting the vices is appropriate for the special concern of the play, since it provides a 'glass' wherein the members of the audience can view the vicious behaviour of which they themselves may be guilty. In *A Looking Glasse*, therefore, the morality elements are present, but they have been adapted to the particular needs of the play.

The fragmented *Misogonus* (c. 1560-1577), possibly written by Laurence Johnson, Thomas Richards, or Anthony Rudd, combines morality elements with those drawn from 'education drama' and Latin comedy.[9] Misogonus, the mankind figure, is in the midst of his life in sin when the play opens. Typically, he is blind to the nature of those who counsel him. He ignores the advice of his father's friend, Eupelas, and the trusty servant, Liturgus. He follows, instead, the evil counsel of the crafty servant Cacurgus and his companions, Oenophilus and Orgelus. Misogonus' fallen state is obvious: his pride is revealed in a scene with the flatterer Orgelus, his lechery is shown in his visit to the prostitute Melissa, and his prodigality is revealed in a long scene of dancing and gambling. He continues in his life of sin until his father decides that he will disown the youth unless he changes his ways and asks his forgiveness. As a result, Misogonus recognizes the evil path he has pursued:

> ...my life hath ben so lewdly ledd, yt I shall neare be wyhout care
> I can haue no mirth but it will be wth miseries continually mixte.[10]

He almost despairs of forgiveness: "I am so ashamed that I dare near come in his [his father's] sighte." (IV, iv, 21) But Liturgus convinces the prodigal that, if he repents, his father will be merciful. The fragmented conclusion suggests that Misogonus does so. He is contrite and evidently confesses his sins; however, as far as we know, he does no penance. The last line"...[spe]ake [from] thy h[ar]te Misogonus my s..." (IV, iv, 47), indicates that the regenerate son does win his father's forgiveness and that, as a result, he is restored to his appropriate place in his father's household.

---

[9] The morality elements in the play have often been noted but not thoroughly examined; for example, see Madeleine Doran, *Endeavors of Art* (Madison: The University of Wisconsin Press, 1963), pp. 162-63.

In brief, the term 'education drama' refers to plays based upon a Biblical source, usually the parable of the prodigal son which was written in Latin and meant to teach schoolboys sound morality as well as Latin grammar and meter. Four plays *Misogonus*, *Nice Wanton*, *The Disobedient Child*, and *The Glasse of Government* are considered by many scholars to be 'education dramas' written in English. All exhibit elements found in the Latin plays. See 'Appendix', which is a short examination of 'education drama'.

[10] *Misogonus*, in *Early Plays from the Italian*, edited by R. Warwick Bond (Oxford, The Clarendon Press, 1911), I, i, 15-16. Other references to the play will be made in the body of the text.

The parable of the prodigal son, important in many 'education dramas', has less influence upon *Misogonus* than we might assume. As in the Biblical tale, Misogonus is the younger of two sons, but the older brother is not discovered until relatively late in the play. Unlike his Biblical prototype, Misogonus does not receive his inheritance or leave his father's home. Finally, while he seeks and receives forgiveness, he undergoes none of the hardships which the prodigal in the *New Testament* account suffers. The evil results of parental indulgence, a frequent concern of 'education drama', are, however, evident in this play. Misogonus is not considered totally responsible for his sinfulness, since his father spoiled him and, consequently, the boy has never been properly trained to follow virtue. Elements found in Latin and neo-Latin comedy are evident in *Misogonus* as well.[11] To cite the major ones, the scene is set in Italy, the names of the characters are derived from Greek, the older son, lost at birth, is recovered, and contrast of loyal and corrupt servants is used. But despite the influence of 'education drama' and Latin comedy, it is clear that the morality pattern provides the play's basic structure and its major formal elements.

The reconciliation of a husband and a wife is the ultimate end in *All's Well That Ends Well* (c. 1601–c. 1604) by Shakespeare. But implicit in this reconciliation is the regeneration of a mankind figure who has fallen from virtue and who, as a result, threatens both his earthly reputation and his spiritual salvation. As several scholars have noticed, despite its novella source, *All's Well* contains numerous morality elements.[12]

The central characters can be grouped according to the morality division. While on one level Helena is a typical patient wife,

---

[11] Miss Doran discusses these; see *Endeavors of Art*, pp. 162–63. The Latin comedy elements are, of course, one means of identifying the play as an 'education drama'.

[12] See, for example, the excellent introduction by G. K. Hunter to Shakespeare's *All's Well That Ends Well* (The Arden Shakespeare, 3rd ed.; London, Methuen and Co., Ltd., 1959), p. lii; E. M. W. Tillyard, *Shakespeare's Problem Plays* (London, Chatto & Windus, 1950), p. 108. Dolora Gallagher Cunningham, "The Doctrine of Repentance as a Formal Principle in Some Elizabethan Plays" (unpublished Ph. D. dissertation, Stanford University, 1953) discusses the elements of repentance but does not discuss other morality elements or see the structure as one drawn from the morality play, pp. 189–206.

anxious to save her husband from his follies, on another she operates as a virtue figure, who brings about Bertram's regeneration.[13] Her curing of the King – as she says, "Heaven hath through me restor'd the king to health" – [14] suggests that she is meant to be considered as a minister of grace, one capable of healing the sick soul as she has healed the sick body.

Opposed to Helena is Parolles, the braggart.[15] His vicious nature is established early by Helena, who says of him:

> ...I know him a notorious liar,
> Think him a great way fool, solely a coward.
> Yet these fix'd evils sit so fit in him
> That they take place when virtue's steely bones
> Looks bleak i' th' cold wind. (I, i, 98–102)

Lafew confirms the validity of her judgment when he later tells Parolles, "The devil it is that's thy master." (II, iii, 245) Such conclusions by those who are clearly just and virtuous serve to identify Parolles with the forces of evil. He certainly functions as a Vice: he encourages Bertram in his life of sin by encouraging him to desert Helena and to disobey the King; later, he plays a willing pander in order to enable Bertram to satisfy his lust for Diana. The depth of his iniquity is revealed fully when he is shown to be a traitor to the army and to his friend as well.

As the term has been defined in this study, Bertram is certainly a typical mankind figure.[16] He is willful and proud, easily tempted by vice but obviously capable of regeneration. His potential worthiness is suggested by his physical resemblance to his father. The King says of him,

---

[13] Hunter calls her a 'minister of grace', p. xxvi; Tillyard says much the same, calling her a representative of 'heavenly grace', p. 108; Mrs. Cunningham sees her as "a representative of redeemed human nature working out of love for the redemption of unredeemed human nature as represented by Bertram", p. 196.

[14] William Shakespeare, *All's Well That Ends Well*, II, iii, 64. Other references to the play will be made in the body of the text.

[15] Hunter states, "Parolles and Helena are arranged on either side of Bertram, placed rather like the Good and Evil Angels in a Morality', *ibid.*, p. xxxiii.

[16] Hunter describes him as "natural man choosing Sin but saved by Grace...", *ibid.*, p. xlvii; Tillyard describes him as 'natural, unredeemed man', p. 108.

> Thy father's moral parts
> Mayst thou inherit too! (I, ii, 21-22)

And his worth is established firmly by Helena's love for him. Bertram's friendship with Parolles, however, indicates that his fall occurred before the play opens and that he is in the midst of his life in sin before his rejection of Helena. His spiritual blindness keeps him from recognizing her worth and leads him, in time, to rebel against the King. As he later confesses:

> At first
> I struck my choice upon her, ere my heart
> Durst make too bold a herald of my tongue;
> Where the impression of mine eye infixing,
> Contempt his scornful perspective did lend me,
> Which warp'd the line of every other favour,
> Scorn'd a fair colour or express'd it stol'n,
> Extended or contracted all proportions
> To a most hideous subject. (V, iii, 44-52)

Bertram is incapable of repenting until his spiritual vision has been improved. He continues in his life in sin, as his lust for Diana shows. His regeneration can begin only after he has seen Parolles for what he is. Clearly, the function of Act III, Scene vi, is to bring this about. As the First Lord tells Bertram, "It were fit you knew him, lest, reposing too far in his virtue, which he hath not, he might at some great and trusty business in a main danger fail you." (III, vi, 13-15)

He is not regenerate, however, until, having recognized his follies, he eschews vice and repents his life in sin. The function of the bed trick and the resulting complicated denouement is, according to Mrs. Cunningham, to make Bertram "...pay for his folly, both actual and intended, through the exposures and humiliations to which he is subject in the last act".[17] His confession occurs in stages: first, that to the King, and then the continuing acknowledgement of his treatment of Diana. The humiliation to which he is subjected can be interpreted as a form of penance for his crimes and, therefore, a means of purification. Contrite, he begs Helena's pardon and promises to lead a virtuous life, symbolized

---

[17] Cunningham, pp. 204-05.

by his promise to love her dearly. Having been forgiven his crimes, he ends as Helena's devoted and beloved husband and as the King's obedient and respected courtier.

*All's Well That Ends Well* employs all of the morality elements except the temptation to despair. While there is no statement of didactic purpose, and the problem of spiritual salvation is never made explicit, this problem exists in the play. For Bertram's intended adultery would result in a sin which would, necessarily, threaten his spiritual well-being. Consequently, although most of the plot machinery is derived from a novella,[18] this machinery is used in *All's Well* to develop a morality-type conflict between Vice and Virtue for the possession of mankind's soul.

Thomas Dekker's *If This Be Not a Good Play, the Devil Is In It* (1611–1612), is the latest of the three morality-patterned comedies dealing with the welfare of a state. It studies the spiritual history of three men, drawn from social ranks upon which the well-being of a realm depends: the Subprior of a religious order, responsible for the spiritual welfare of the citizens; Bartervile, a usurious merchant, who affects those with whom he has commerce; and the King of Naples, who provides a model of virtue or vice for his subjects to follow. Although its didactic intention is never made explicit, the play clearly deals with the problem of man's spiritual salvation.

It opens with the introduction of the Vices. Pluto decides to send three devils, Shacklesoule, Rufman, and Lurchall, to earth to obtain the souls of the priests, the king, and the city dwellers. The devils are certain of success and promise him that, "Thou shalt be forc'd to enlarge thy Iayle of Hell."[19] Their success, however, rests entirely upon the spiritual condition of the men they tempt. The avaricious Bartervile immediately accepts the help of Lurchall, and, indeed, is so corrupt that the devil admits, "I came to teach, but now (me thinkes) must learne." (IV, i, 85) Bartervile, of course,

---

[18] The source has generally been assumed to be Painter's *Palace of Pleasure*, which translates the ninth novel of the third day of the *Decameron*. It is possible, however, that a translation by le Macon is the immediate source. Hunter discusses the problems of source, pp. xxv–xxix.

[19] Thomas Dekker, *If This Be Not a Good Play, the Devil Is In It*, in *The Dramatic Works of Thomas Dekker*, edited by Fredson Bowers, III (Cambridge, The University Press, 1958), I, i, 138. Other references to the play will be made in the body of the text.

is ultimately sent to Hell. Shacklesoule's task, the downfall of a monastery, seems easy enough to achieve. Pretending to be Friar Rush, he has little difficulty in convincing most of his 'brothers' that their lives are unnecessarily austere. But he fails to tempt the virtuous Subprior, the one man whose soul he most desires.

The King of Naples, the type of traditional mankind figure we have been examining in this study, begins in a state of virtue: as a new ruler, he is determined to be just and wise. But blinded by Rifman's flattery he soon accepts the devil as his confidant. Having fallen, the King becomes proud, lecherous, avaricious, and tyrannical. Despite the advice of his uncle Octavio, who functions as a virtue figure in the struggle for Naples' soul, the King follows the counsel of Rufman and his other flatterers. Finally, he becomes involved in a disastrous war. Believing it lost and encouraged by Rufman, the desperate King is tempted to commit suicide, an act which would result, of course, in his damnation. The King is saved, however, from such an act by a vision of hell, after which he repents. His repentance is not portrayed fully, but it is represented by his regret for his sins and his request for divine mercy:

> My soule was sunck too low, to looke more hye,
> Forgiuenes heauen. (V, i, 71-72)

He does no penance. But once he repents, his spiritual vision improves. Although he does not realize that Rufman is, in fact, a devil, the King no longer trusts him. With divine help, as a sign that he is forgiven, the regenerate king reverses the tides of war and wins the battle. The victorious and virtuous ruler banishes his evil counsellors from the court, rights the wrongs of his subjects, and promises:

> Here we begin
> Our reigne anew, which golden threds shall spin,
> Iustice shall henceforth sit vpon our throne,
> And vertue be your Kings companion. (V, iii, 156-59)

Despite a final scene portraying the sufferings of the damned, the development of the action culminates with the regeneration of the King of Naples, a mankind figure, and with his return to a state of virtue.

As this brief summary suggests, *If This Be Not a Good Play* has the morality didactic intention and employs all the formal elements. But the repentance of the mankind figure is contracted greatly and penance is omitted. In addition, the play adds two types, the Subprior and the usurer, in order to express more adequately its concern with the welfare of a nation.

Six comedies contain two variations in the morality pattern. *Histrio-mastix* (1589-1599), revised by John Marston, *The Wise-Woman of Hogsdon* (c. 1604?), by Thomas Heywood, *Match Me in London* (c. 1611-c. 1613), by Thomas Dekker, and *The Lady of Pleasure* (1635), by James Shirley, omit the temptation to despair. *Histrio-mastix*, *Match Me in London*, *The Staple of News* (1626), by Ben Jonson, and *The Lady of Pleasure* omit penance. The elimination of the vice or the use of minor characters as vice figures occurs in *The Wise-Woman*, *The London Prodigal*, and *The Staple of News*. *The London Prodigal* (1603-1604) varies the point of repentance.

*Histrio-mastix*, the third of the political comedies to be discussed, is the earliest of the plays in this group. It is the only one to employ several mankind figures, from various segments of society, and to open with them in a state of virtue. As do the majority of morality-patterned comedies, the remaining plays employ a single mankind figure, open with him in the midst of his life in sin, and deal only with his private affairs. In *The London Prodigal*, *The Staple of News*, and *The Lady of Pleasure*, the predominant sin to which the mankind figure succumbs is prodigality; in *The Wise-Woman* and *Match Me in London*, it is lust. In *Match Me in London*, the mankind figure is a king; in *The Lady of Pleasure*, the mankind figure is the wife of a lord; in the other plays, he is of less than noble rank.

The anonymous *Histrio-mastix* (1589-1599), which was revised by John Marston, is well known to students of Renaissance drama because of the information it contains about Elizabethan theatre. As Muriel Bradbrook points out, however, the work employs "a strong morality structure."[20] Yet some scholars have ignored the

---

[20] Muriel Bradbrook states that the play "...has a strong morality structure, in which the ruin of Respublica is the theme". (p. 97) However, she never defines the term 'morality structure' and she states later that, "The structure of the old moral play is most closely reflected

presence of morality elements in the play. For example, E. K. Chambers states: "The theme is the cyclical progression of a state through the stages Peace, Plenty, Pride, Envy, War, Poverty and Peace again."[21] While there is no question that *Histrio-mastix* follows this cyclical progression, nevertheless, the progression itself depends upon the moral condition of the inhabitants of the state. Chrisoganus, the primary virtue figure and the one citizen who does not succumb to sensual temptations, makes it clear that Respublica's downfall was the result of sin; as he states, by studying the arts and

> By nursing them in Peace I shun'd all Sloth;
> Nor yet did Plenty make me prodigall:
> Pride I abhor'd, and term'd the Beggers shield;
> Nor ever did base Envie touch my heart;
> . . . . . . . . . . . . . . . . . . .
> Nor could the ratling fury of fierce warre
> Astonish me more than the mid-night clock,
> The Trumpetter to Contemplation.[22]

The other citizens, unlike Chrisoganus, pursued sensual pleasures and so brought ruin to themselves and to their nation. The well-being of a state, then, depends upon its inhabitants. When they are virtuous, the nation is a land of peace and plenty, but when they are sinful, it is beset by war, chaos, and poverty.

*Histrio-mastix*, therefore, is concerned primarily with the problem of man's earthly happiness. But fused with this problem is that of man's spiritual well-being. As in the Tudor moral interludes, the two are handled as one. The citizen seeking earthly happiness must contribute to the peace and prosperity of his state by living virtuously. When he does so, he works, at the same time, toward his spiritual salvation. A few speeches reflect the fusion of the

---

in the later comedies of Jonson, especially *The Devil is an Ass* and *The Magnetic Lady;* but it is most powerfully and successfully present in the characterization of Volpone." (p. 227) In my opinion, none of these plays employ the morality structure or morality elements.

[21] E. K. Chambers, *The Elizabethan Stage* (Oxford, The Clarendon Press, 1923) IV, 18.

[22] *Histrio-mastix*, in *The School of Shakespeare*, edited by Richard Simpson, II (London, Chatto and Windus, 1878), VI, i, 112–116 and 118–120. Other references to the play will be made in the body of the text.

two problems. Chrisoganus, for example, laments that Envy has engulfed the nation:

> Oh, I could curse
> This idiot world, this ill-nurst age of Peace,
> That foster[s] all save virtue; comforts all
> Saving industrious art, the souls bright gemme. (IV, i, 135-38)

Later he states that because of

> Vile Ambition, Pitty and Piety are both exilde,
> Religion buried with our Fathers bones,
> In the cold earth, and nothing but her face
> Left to adorne these gross and impious times. (V, i, 143-46)

The play teaches, we may conclude, that for man to achieve earthly happiness and spiritual salvation he must eschew vice, repent his sins, and live virtuously.

In *Histrio-mastix*, pursuit of knowledge is offered as the best way for men to live virtuously and for the state to remain prosperous. The Arts, Grammar, Logic, Rhetoric, Arithmetic, Geometry, Music, and Astronomy

> ...are adjuncts fit to waite on Peace,
> Who beeing courted by most searching spirits,
> Have alwayes borne themselves in God-like state
> With lofty fore heads, higher then the starres. (I, i, 9-12)

While the structure follows generally that of the morality, there are some variations. As in the Tudor interludes, the introduction of the Vices, is omitted. The play opens instead with the introduction of Peace and the Arts, who establish the importance of learning to the well-being of a state and its inhabitants.

The mankind figures are then introduced in a state of virtue. As in *A Looking Glasse* and because of the play's special concern, numerous mankind figures are employed. Rather than consider them all and in order to facilitate this discussion, the lords will be used to illustrate the play's morality pattern.

When the play opens, the lords and the nation are in a state of virtue, represented by the ascendancy of the liberal arts and by the country's peaceful and prosperous condition. Each lord chooses to study one particular art, while Chrisoganus, the most virtuous, chooses to study them all. Eventually, however, the lords weary of pursuing knowledge, become slothful, and seek sensual pleasures. As Mavortius says,

> I cannot feed my appetite with Ayre
> I must pursue my pleasures royally:
> ...And leave this Idle contemplation
> To rugged Stoicall Morosophists. (II, i, 51-51; 55-56)

The reason for their fall is not given, but once they have fallen, the lords become blind to virtue. Mavortius, for example, dismisses his loyal servants so that,

> A thousand pound a yeare will so be sav'd,
> For revelling and banquetting and playes. (III, i, 119-20)

Like the rest of the nation, the lords become proud, envious, and ambitious, and, consequently, after a disastrous war, become impoverished. Their poverty, however, serves to correct their spiritual vision. For they recognize in adversity what they did not recognize in prosperity, that the pleasures they sought endangered their well-being. As Philarchus says,

> My full-mouthd bags may now be fild with ayre,
> The Divell and Ambition taught it me. (VI, i, 50-51)

They are not tempted to despair, and their repentance is not as fully portrayed as it is in other plays. But it is suggested by their sorrow for and their admission of their sins and by their desire to seek the counsel of Chrisoganus, from whom they wish to know:

> How might we tread the path's to happy ends,
> Since foes to Learning are not Vertues friends? (VI, i, 123-24)

They do no penance. But because they are now regenerate, peace and plenty are restored to them and to their nation.

The characters in *Histrio-mastix* can be separated into three groups. The Vices are presented in two ways. Some, for example, Pride, Vaine-Glory, and Ambition, are allegorical figures. Others are revealed only through the actions of the mankind figures. Sloth, for example, is indicated when Mavortius and Philarchus abandon their studies, and prodigality is revealed when their wives buy extravagant jewelry and clothes. The Virtues, also, are presented in two ways. The liberal arts are allegorical figures, who appear in the first scene. But throughout most of the play, Chrisoganus, the one man who does not fall, functions as the major virtue figure. He comments upon the moral significance of the action, and once the state has been brought to ruin because of vice, he teaches the lords how to follow the path of virtue.

The third group consists of the inhabitants of the nation. Unregenerate man is represented by the Players, who flourish when the nation is immersed in sin, but who, once the citizens have rejected sensual pleasures, are banished because they are incapable of redemption. The virtuous man, incapable of succumbing to temptation, is represented by Chrisoganus. Between these extremes lie the representatives of typical humanity, well-meaning but easily tempted. These include the Lords Mavortius, Philarchus, Larius, and Hiletus, and, to a lesser extent, the citizens Fourcher, Velure, Lyonrash, Champtery, and Calamanca. The use of so many characters provides a cross-section of representative classes and types.

How the morality pattern has been varied in *Histrio-mastix* is clear from the preceding discussion. These variations serve, of course, the particular needs of the play. For they provide a vivid dramatization of the steps by which the peace and the prosperity of a nation can be destroyed and the ways in which they can be restored.

When *The London Prodigal* (1603-1604) opens, Matthew Flowerdale, the mankind figure, has already fallen into a life of sin. He is a wastrel, a debtor, and a gambler. At first, his father treats the boy's wantonness lightly; for he believes that his son will soon perceive his vices and turn from them:

For vice once looked into with the eyes of discretion, and well balanced with the weights of reason, the course passed seems so abhominable, that the landlord of himself, which is the heart of his body, will rather entomb himself in the earth, or seek a new tenant to remain in him; which once settled, how much better are they that in their youth have known all these vices, and left them, than those that knew little, and in their age run into them ?[23]

---

[23] *The London Prodigal*, in *The Doubtful Plays of William Shakespeare*, edited by William Hazlitt (London, George Routledge and Sons, 1887), p. 207. Other references to the play will be made in the body of the text.

After giving out the news that he is dead and that Matthew is disinherited, the father disguises himself and becomes Matthew's servant in order to observe his son's behavior. He soon learns that his tolerance was foolish. As his father says, the youth is

> ...heedless as a libertine;
> Even grown a master in the school of vice:
> One that doth nothing, but invent deceit. (p. 227)

In an abortive attempt to bring about Matthew's regeneration, the father has him arrested for debt on his wedding day. In order to evade the police, Matthew abandons his wife, taking her dowry as funds for gambling. Once he has gambled this money away, the penniless prodigal becomes desperate and, for a moment, contemplates suicide: "I have passed the very utmost bounds of shifting; I have no course now but to hange myself." (p. 240) He decides, instead, to beg.

Through his misfortune, Matthew's spiritual vision is improved, and he realizes, for the first time, that his companions in vice were actually his enemies:

> They give me counsel that first cozen'd me.
> Those devils first brought me to the thing I am,
> And being thus, the first that do me wrong. (p. 240)

But this realization does not bring about his repentance, as it does that of the other mankind figures we have studied. His wife disappears. Suspected of having murdered her, Matthew is arrested and sentenced to die. But he is saved from execution by her sudden reappearance. Moved by her extraordinary virtue and her love for him, he now repents:

> Thy chastity and virtue hath infused
> Another soul in me, red with defame,
> For in my blushing cheeks is seen my shame. (p. 245)

His contrition is indicated by his admission of shame; his confession is implied here and in his general request for pardon from his father and from others he has wronged. His trial serves, as it does in *How a Man May Chuse*, as a form of penance, through which he suffers for his crimes. At the end of the play, the regenerate

Matthew has been forgiven by his father and restored to his proper place as beloved son and husband.

Although the play employs the full morality pattern, two elements are varied significantly enough to deserve notice. The virtue figures, Matthew's father and his wife, are major characters, important for the development of the action. The vice figures, on the other hand, although they do appear briefly, are minor characters, less important than in most morality-patterned comedies. In this play, they have nothing to do with the development of the action; they merely serve to demonstrate the hypocrisy of sinful companions who, though pretending friendship, invariably desert the man in need. Usually, the repentance of the mankind figure comes immediately after his recognition that he has followed a life of sin. But in *The London Prodigal*, it is delayed until the last possible moment so that the resolution of the plot results, as well, in the moment of highest emotional intensity, when the joyful husband, having just been saved from death by his virtuous wife, repents and promises to amend.

Heywood's *The Wise-Woman of Hogsdon* (c. 1604?) combines morality elements with elements derived from Latin comedy. It begins with Chartley, the mankind figure, in the midst of his life in sin. He is shown to be both prodigal and lustful, but it is the latter weakness upon which the plot depends. This lust is revealed by a soliloquy in which he relates his desire to seduce Luce I: "But the fool stands in her own light, and will do nothing without marriage. But what should I do marrying?"[24] To obtain her and at the same time to be able to deny her as his wife, he convinces Luce I to participate in a secret marriage at the home of the wise-woman. By marrying her, however, he would break his vow to Luce II, whom he deserted when he came to London. The secret marriage is the means by which Chartley's intended crimes are not realized. Luce II takes Luce I's place and so is married to Chartley without his knowledge. When Chartley refuses to make the marriage public and becomes betrothed to the wealthy Gratina, he is saved from possible adultery by Luce II, who contrives to

---

[24] Thomas Heywood, *The Wise-Woman of Hogsdon*, in *Thomas Heywood*, edited by A. Wilson Verity, Vol. I ("The Mermaid Series"; London, Vizetelly and Co., 1888), I, i, p. 257. Other references to the play will be made in the body of the text.

force Chartley's open confession of his sins and his repentance. On the evening of his second marriage, pretending to be Luce I, she writes him a note, asking him to meet her at the wise-woman's and she convinces Gratina to go there at the same time in order to buy a dress.

The last scene is an extremely complicated unraveling of the plot so that appropriate husbands are found for the deceived Luce I and Gratina and so that all of Chartley's sins are revealed. He is humiliated by the airing of his intended crimes, is forced to admit to each, and receives the general scorn of all present. He is, as a result, made to see himself as he is. Recognizing his fallen state, he turns from it:

> Then see, sir: when to all your judgments I see me past grace, do I lay hold of grace, and here begin to retire myself. This woman hath lent me a glass, in which I see all my imperfections, at which my conscience doth more blush inwardly than my face outwardly; and now I dare confidently undertake for myself I am honest. (V, iv, p. 325)

He is not tempted to despair. His contrition is obvious in the above speech, and he confesses both specifically and generally throughout the scene. His penance, however, like that of Bertram in *All's Well*, is achieved through the humiliations he undergoes for his sins of intention. That he has changed is demonstrated by his promise to amend and by his joyful recognition of Luce II, his first love. The regenerate Chartley is forgiven by those he has wronged and restored to his appropriate place as a beloved son, friend, and husband.

Chartley is certainly a typical mankind figure. Once virtuous, he has been tempted by his London companions and has fallen into a life of sin. He is, nevertheless, capable of regeneration. The primary virtue character is Luce II, his forsaken fiancée. Her manipulations prevent Chartley from accomplishing his intended crimes and compel him to admit them publicly. There is, however, no vice figure. The wise-woman might be considered a Vice because she allows Chartley to use her house for his sinful schemes, but since she joins in the plot to defeat those very schemes and to help Luce II, she does not fulfill a Vice's function.

Combined with morality elements are others drawn from Latin comedy. The complicated plot, for example, depends upon manipulation. And as in Latin comedy, the resolution is achieved because the manipulator himself is tricked. The plot, moreover, centers in courtship, albeit Chartley's courtship of three women. His attempt to seduce Luce I, a shopgirl, is reminiscent of a favorite New Comedy theme – the love of a young man for a woman who is an unsuitable match. It determines many of the plot complications. The disguises also are probably derived from Latin comedy. The combination of Latin comedy elements with the morality pattern indicates once again what has been demonstrated elsewhere, particularly in *How a Man May Chuse:* that the morality-patterned comedy reflects the influences of other types of drama.

Thomas Dekker's *Match Me in London* (c. 1611–c. 1613) centers, primarily, in the testing of Tormiella, a virtuous wife, but it employs all but two of the morality elements. The King of Spain can be considered a mankind figure. He is so obsessed by lust that he threatens his spiritual welfare, his life, and, potentially, the welfare of his state. There are two vice figures: Lady Dildoman and Lupo (the disguised Gazetto, a rejected suitor of Tormiella). The first is the King's former mistress and now his bawd; she is "...a Lady Pandresse, and (as this years Almanacke sayes) has a priuate hot-house for his Grace onely to sweat in".[25] Lupo attaches himself to the King and encourages Spain's pursuit of Tormiella. The primary virtue figure is Tormiella. Despite the temptations the King offers her, she rejects his advances and so keeps him from fulfilling his sinful desire. It is she, furthermore, who brings about his repentance when she reveals the plot to murder him.

The play begins with the King of Spain in the midst of his life in sin. From Lady Dildoman, he learns of Tormiella, the virtuous wife of Cordolente. When she refuses to become his mistress, the King decides to have his wife murdered so that he will be free to marry her. Obsessed by lust, he is blind to the worth of his counsellors and the potential consequences of his acts. He accepts

---

[25] Thomas Dekker, *Match Me in London*, in *The Dramatic Works of Thomas Dekker*, edited by Fredson Bowers, III (Cambridge, The University Press, 1958), I, iv, 100–01. Other references to the play will be made in the body of the text.

According to its title page, the play is called a 'tragi-comedy'. As I have stated in Chapter I, however, the term is often ambiguous. Here, it probably refers to the station of the king. At any rate, I felt free to include it with the morality patterned comedies since I felt it was closer to these works than to other types of Renaissance drama.

Lupo as his servant only to discover later that Lupo had conspired against him. And he accuses the loyal soldier, Martines, of treason. By his treatment of the queen, Spain angers his father-in-law, who joins in a conspiracy to usurp the throne. Spain's attempt to corrupt Cordolente and Tormiella's father by ennobling them if he can so win the girl shows that he will ignore all his responsibilities to fulfill his lust. And this lust is common knowledge in his kingdom (IV, iii, 10-27). Since a king leads his subjects in virtue or in vice, the welfare of the state is threatened by his sinfulness.

Spain's lust almost brings about his death; for if forced to marry the King, Tormiella would have murdered him on their wedding night. The marriage ceremony, fortunately, is stopped by Cordolente. While begging for her husband's life, Tormiella discloses the plot against the King. Spain's spiritual vision is corrected immediately. He recognizes the true natures of Lupo and Lady Dildoman and his own sinfulness. Although he is not tempted to despair, he does repent. Contrite, he confesses:

> Rare Prouidence, I thanke thee, what a heape
> Of mischiefes haue I brought vpon my Kingdome,
> By one base Act of lust, and my greatest horror
> Is that for her I made away my Queene. (V, v, 24-27)

He does no penance. His wife, who was not actually killed, appears and forgives her husband his ill treatment of her. And his brother, who had led the conspiracy to usurp the throne, appears and promises, henceforth, to be a loyal subject. The King of Spain ends, therefore, as a virtuous man, a virtuous husband, and a virtuous ruler of a united kingdom. As this brief investigation suggests, *Match Me in London* weaves various threads – the intrigues of the court, the revenge of a disappointed lover, the testing of a patient wife, and the spiritual corruption of a king – into a complicated and loosely constructed plot, for which the morality elements provide at least one source of dramatic coherence.

Ben Jonson's *The Staple of News* (1626)[26] is both a comedy dealing with the adventures of a prodigal and a dramatization of the

---

[26] Many scholars have noticed that the play is indebted to the morality, but none has analyzed the extent. For example, see L. C. Knights, *Drama and Society in the Age of Jonson* (London, Chatto & Windus, 1937), p. 191; Bradbrook, pp. 47-48; and Doran, pp. 164-65.

contention between covetousness, prodigality, and liberality for the control of money.

The work opens with Young Pennyboy, a prodigal mankind figure, in the midst of his life in sin. His father, who functions as a virtue figure, has disguised himself and acts as his son's servant in order to observe the boy's behavior. At the beginning of the play, Pennyboy reveals his excessive pride, indicated by his excessive concern with his physical appearance. His sinfulness makes him deaf to his father's wise counsel and blind to the fact that he is surrounded by flatterers and fools. It leads him to buy Tom, a barber, a place in the absurd Staple of News. His follies continue to increase until he finally mistreats Pecunia, his fiancée. In righteous anger, his father takes off his disguise and disinherits his son, save for a patched cloak.

After he has been disinherited, and for the first time, Young Pennyboy sees himself for what he is, a prodigal surrounded by foolish companions. He almost despairs of restoring his fortunes. His contrition is suggested in the soliloquy where he confesses his faults:

> I now begin to see my vanity
> Shine in this Glasse, reflected by the foile ![27]

He does no penance. Instead, in order to win his father's forgiveness, he proves that he has mended his ways. Pretending to help Picklock obtain the deed which insures his inheritance, Pennyboy unmasks the fradulent lawyer. As a result, he is reconciled with his father and restored to his appropriate position as a beloved son and the worthy suitor of Pecunia. He ends a wise and wealthy man, for his repentant avaricious uncle leaves him

> ...my house, goods, lands, all but my vices,
> And those I goe to cleanse. (V, vi, 55-56)

*The Staple of News* demonstrates thoroughly the earthly rewards of eschewing vice, repenting one's sins, and embracing virtue. The problem of man's spiritual well-being, while not stressed, is

---

[27] Ben Jonson, *The Staple of News*, in *Ben Jonson*, edited by C. H. Herford and Percy Simpson, VI (Oxford, The Clarendon Press, 1932), V, i, 14-15. Other references to the play will be made in the body of the text.

suggested by the uncle's reference to cleansing his vices and by Pecunia's concluding address to the audience; she states that men should use money as an aid:

> Not slaue vnto their pleasures, or a Tyrant
> Ouer their faire desires; but to teach them all
> The golden meane; the Prodigall how to liue,
> The sordid, and the couetous, how to dye:
> That with sound mind; this, safe frugality. (V, vi, 63-67)

Since prodigality and covteousness are different aspects of the same sin, this speech summarizes the didactic intention of the play. If man is to achieve earthly happiness and spiritual salvation, he must follow the golden mean. In *The Staple of News*, then, Jonson employs morality elements not only to tell the tale of the prodigal reclaimed, but, in addition, to settle the contention between covetousness, prodigality, and liberality over the handling of earthly wealth.

Shirley's *The Lady of Pleasure* (1635), the latest of the morality-patterned comedies, satirizes the manners of London society. It is composed of two plots of equal importance: one dealing with the courtship of Celestina and Lord A, and the other, from which the title is derived, dealing with the regeneration of Aretina Bornwell, a prodigal wife. As George Sensabaugh has shown, the two are contrasted. The Celestina plot offers not only a satire of manners but, as well, "...an exposition of Platonic love and its effects upon those who practice its rites and live by its tenets".[28] The Aretina plot, on the other hand, exposes the folly of living for sensual pleasures. In order to do so, it draws upon all but two of the morality elements.

When the play opens, Aretina Bornwell, the mankind figure, is in the midst of her life in sin. Corrupted by her London companions, she is an excessively proud and foolish woman, who spends fortunes on her wardrobe, entertainment, and gambling excursions. That she has fallen from a state of virtue is established in the first scene, when her steward describes her former country life:

---

[28] George F. Sensabaugh, "Platonic Love in Shirley's *The Lady of Pleasure*", *A Tribute to George Coffin Taylor*, edited by Arnold Williams (Richmond, Virginia, The University of North Carolina Press by The William Byrd Press, 1952), p. 177.

You liv'd there
Secure, and innocent, beloved of all;
Prais'd for your hospitality, and pray'd for:
You might be envied; but malice knew
Not where you dwelt.[29]

The case is altered, now:

> We do not [now] invite the poor o' the parish
> To dinner, keep a table for the tenants;...
> . . . . . . . . . . . . . . . . .
> Now make my lady merry. We do feed
> Like princes, and feast nothing [else] but princes. (p. 28)

She is blind to her own sins and blind to the natures of her unworthy companions: Lady Decoy, the major vice figure, who first introduced her to prodigal pleasures; the foolish gallant Littleworth; and the seducer Kickshaw. Consequently, she considers her husband's condemnation of her prodigality and her companions to be the result of avarice.

Lord Bornwell, who functions as a virtue figure, decides to force his wife to change her life by offering her his own riotous example. He pretends that he would rather,

> Be lord one month of pleasures, to the height
> And rapture of our senses, than be years
> Consuming what we have in foolish temperance. (p. 74)

To some extent, the ruse works, for Aretina begins to realize that,

> If we both waste so fast, we shall soon find
> Our state is not immortal. Something in
> His other ways appear not ill already. (p. 82)

Aretina does not repent until she is forced to recognize her sinfulness. She commits adultery with Kickshaw, and, ironically, it is he who leads her to turn from vice. Because she disguised herself during the tryst, he does not recognize Aretina to be his secret mistress. To amuse her, he confides the details of that tryst,

---

[29] James Shirley, *The Lady of Pleasure*, in *The Dramatic Works and Poems of James Shirley*, edited by William Gifford (London: John Murray, 1833), IV, 6. Other references to the play will be made in the body of the text.

describing his mistress as a she-devil. She immediately recognizes her moral deformity. Looking at herself in a mirror, she cries,

> 'Tis a false glass; sure I am more deform'd:
> What have I done? — my soul is miserable. (p. 92)

She is not tempted to despair. But once her image of herself has been corrected, the contrite wife confesses the sin of prodigality to her husband:

> Heaven has dissolved the clouds that hung upon
> My eyes, and if you can with mercy meet
> A penitent, I throw my own will off,
> And now in all things obey your's. (p. 98)

For the sin of adultery, she begs divine forgiveness only:

> Pardon, heaven,
> My shame, yet hid from the world's eye. (p. 99)

She does no penance. Having been forgiven by her husband, she learns from him that her prodigality has not seriously affected her prosperity. The regenerate wife agrees to return to the country where she will be safe from the sensual temptations that London offers. The Aretina plot in *The Lady of Pleasure*, then, utilizes morality elements to satirize the dangers of urban life, where all too easily the virtuous may be enticed to pursue the sins of the flesh.

The last two plays to be discussed are on the periphery of the category of morality-patterned comedies. They include, however, enough elements to be considered. The Second Part of *The Honest Whore* (1604–c. 1605), by Thomas Dekker, has fewer morality elements than the First Part. It omits the vice character and the temptation to despair. Furthermore, while Matheo, the mankind figure, repents, the portrayal of his repentance is severely contracted. In general, *The Miseries of Enforced Marriage* (1605–1606), by George Wilkins, employs the morality pattern. But it omits the vice and virtue characters and varies the mankind figure's attitude toward his life in sin, and the point of his repentance. Both plays employ mankind figures of less than noble rank who succumb to the sin of prodigality. *The Honest Whore* opens with the mankind figure in the midst of his life in sin, while *The Miseries of Enforced Marriage* opens with him in a state of virtue.

The main plot of the Second Part of Thomas Dekker's *The Honest Whore* (1604–c. 1605) has fewer morality elements than the First Part has. In the sequel, Bellafront becomes a typical virtuous wife and much of the play is devoted to the testing of her virtue. Hippolito's role is reversed, and he now acts as the tempter, who tries unsuccessfully to seduce the honest whore. Matheo is made into the mankind figure, a typical prodigal husband, who gambles, rejects his wife, and, finally, commits theft. His trial results in his regeneration. Because his virtuous wife pleads for him, Orlando, Bellafront's father, clears Matheo of the charge of theft. Matheo's repentance, however, is not dramatized but is merely suggested by his comment that since his father-in law has 'the true Phisicion plaid', he is 'now his Patient'.[30] He does no penance. Forgiveness for his sins is indicated when Orlando blesses both Bellafront and Matheo and saves them from poverty by making them his heirs.

The Second Part of *The Honest Whore* is much less original than the First Part. The First Part is an exceptional work because it deals with the regeneration of a courtesan. Ordinarily, in Renaissance drama and particularly in the morality-patterned comedies, the courtesan is an evil character, considered to be so depraved that she is incapable of being redeemed.[31] Like so many Renaissance plays, including some morality-patterned comedies, and despite its references to Bellafront's past, the Second Part deals conventionally with a much more common subject, the regeneration of a prodigal husband and the testing of a patient wife. The sequel, consequently, is a less interesting work.

As its title suggests, George Wilkins' *The Miseries of Enforced Marriage* (1605–1606) is a social thesis play which attacks the convention of arranged marriages. The effectiveness of its argument, however, is weakened by the morality structure upon which the dramatic organization depends.

William Scarborow, the central character and the mankind figure, begins in a state of virtue. He is, as his guardian informs us,

---

[30] Thomas Dekker, *The Honest Whore, Part II*, in *The Dramatic Works of Thomas Dekker*, Vol. II, V, iii, 191–92.

[31] The subject of a courtesan's regeneration has a long and honorable tradition. It is based, of course, upon the lives of converted courtesans such as Saint Thais and Saint Mary of Egypt, and has its ultimate roots in the Biblical account of Mary Magdalene.

> ...A noble branch, increasing blessed fruit,
> Where caterpillar vice dare not to touch:
> He bears himself with so much gravity,
> Praise cannot praise him with hyperpole.[32]

His fall results from his enforced marriage. Though betrothed to Clare, against his will Scarborow weds Katherine, the choice of his guardian. By arranging a marriage for his ward, his guardian initiates the conflict which leads to Scarborow's downfall; but the youth himself is to some extent responsible for his misery. He became engaged secretly to Clare who was not a wholly suitable match. He deserts her because, when forced to choose between his betrothal vows and his birthright, he is incapable of giving up his inheritance. Essentially, then, the choice which Scarborow faces is the same choice which faces any mankind figure, that is, the choice between the spiritual and the sensual good; for Scarborow is tempted by the threat of poverty to break sacred vows. Unwilling to lose his inheritance, the means by which he can satisfy his sensual desires, he betrays his beloved and, consequently, threatens his spiritual welfare.

Scarborow's life in sin begins soon after his marriage. Overwhelmed by remorse because of Clare's suicide, he becomes a prodigal. While most mankind figures are blind to their sinful state, Scarborow not only recognizes his moral condition but purposely seeks evil companions and an evil life:

> Thus like a fever that doth shake a man
> From strength to weakness, I consume myself.
> I know this company, their custom vile,
> Hated, abhorr'd of good men, yet like a child
> By reason's rule, instructed how to know
> Evil from good, I to the worser go. (p. 512)

He wastes his inheritance, and that of his siblings. He even disowns his wife and children. Finally, he becomes desperate:

---

[32] George Wilkins, *The Miseries of Enforced Marriage*, in *A Select Collection of Old English Plays*, edited by W. Carew Hazlitt (4th ed.; London, Reeves and Turner, 1874), IX, 482. Other references to the play will be made in the body of the text. The character and situation of William Scarborow are based upon the history of William Calvary, whose murder of his children is the subject of *A Yorkshire Tragedy*.

> ...I find spendthrifts (and such am I)
> Like strumpets flourish, but are foul within,
> And they (like snakes) know when to cast their skin. (p. 554)

Regretting what he has done, Scarborow repents, confessing to his brother that he has sinned and showing that he is contrite:

> If penitence your losses might repair,
> You should be rich in wealth, and I in care. (p. 556)

Although his repentance is not accepted by his brother, evidently it is heard in Heaven, and brings about divine intervention which saves Scarborow from certain damnation. Just as he is about to murder his wife and children he is stopped because he learns that his guardian, regretting his former treatment of his ward, has died and made him his heir. The prodigal thanks God, "That gives men comfort as he gives his rod" (p. 575), and begs and receives the forgiveness of those he has wronged. Though he does no penance, he does pay the portions he owes his brother and sister. Ironically, he ends wealthier than he was at the time the play opened, since his guardian has left him a sum greater than that of his original inheritance. The regenerate Scarborow promises, to be, thereafter, a virtuous husband and brother.

While some morality elements, particularly the morality structure, are present, the play contains several variations. Unlike other mankind figures, Scarborow's spiritual vision is clear throughout his life in sin, and though he is contrite and confesses, he does no penance. The play differs, furthermore, because it has no vice or virtue figures. In a sense, we may say that their functions are combined in the behaviour of Scarborow's guardian. As does a Vice, he tempts his ward, here by threatening him with disinheritance. But despite the results of his act, his intentions are unlike those of a Vice, for he believes that Katherine would be a more suitable match and that Scarborow is stopped from committing murder only because he learns that his guardian has left him his wealth. With this money, he is able to obtain the forgiveness of those he has wronged by making restitution and to become the virtuous husband and father he now desires to be.

*The Miseries of Enforced Marriage* is obviously an attempt to examine and to comment upon a contemporary social problem: the control of a guardian over the life of his ward. It attacks the arranged marriage by showing that such a marriage can lead to great misery. But the force of its social criticism is weakened because the work depends upon the morality structure for much of its dramatic organization. This means that by the end of the play the mankind figure must repent, must be forgiven his crimes, and must be restored to his appropriate place in society. For the morality structure we have been examining requires a happy ending, no matter how improbable it may be. So at the conclusion of the play and despite the enforced marriage, Scarborow, a typically regenerate mankind figure, appears certain to be a virtuous and contented husband and father.

The Renaissance plays examined in this chapter at first might seem to have little in common, since they were written by various playwrights at various times throughout the late sixteenth and early seventeenth centuries. But as we have seen, they do, in fact, have a great deal in common. For they all employ formal elements found in the morality play and they depend upon the morality structure for their dramatic organization.

Obviously, all of them are placed firmly in a Christian universe and are based upon orthodox Christian dogma. And they all have a particular didactic intention, be it explicit or implicit. As in the Tudor moral interludes, this didactic intention is two-fold: to show man how to achieve earthly happiness and spiritual salvation. The means of attaining both ends, however, is the same. By eschewing vice, repenting his sins, and living virtuously, man fulfills his social responsibilities and so insures his earthly happiness at the same time as he works in the best possible manner toward the salvation of his soul. *The Faire Maide* will illustrate. Seeking to satisfy his lust, Vallenger ignores his marital duties, and, in so doing, he brings about his own unhappiness and almost brings about his death. Since lust is a sin, by embracing it, Vallenger necessarily threatens his spiritual well-being. Conversely, when he repents and promises to become a dutiful husband and a virtuous man, he obtains earthly joy and indicates that he will live as a Christian must who is concerned about his eternal life.

The two-fold didactic intention is reflected in the action of the morality-patterned comedy. On one level, the action centers in the conflict between those who encourage the mankind figure to avoid his social and Christian responsibilities and those who try to make him fulfill them. The companions of a prodigal, for instance, encourage his riotous behaviour, while the virtuous father or wife seeks to make him realize the folly of his ways. On another level, however, it deals with the same conflict found in the older English morality and the Tudor interludes examined: the conflict between the Vices and the Virtues for the possession of mankind's soul. To cite one example, if the Dutch courtesan had succeeded in enticing Malheureux into committing murder, she would not only have achieved her revenge, but, in addition, she would have threatened Malheureux's spiritual salvation. Frevill, on the other hand, manipulated in order to defeat the courtesan's schemes, to bring about his friend's repentance and, consequently, to help him achieve spiritual salvation.

In addition to a two-fold didactic intention, the seventeen plays making up the morality-patterned comedy exhibit other developments which can be traced to the Tudor moral interlude. In these plays, as in all but three of the Tudor interludes, the morality pattern is adapted to one particular incident and one particular subject. *Wyt and Science*, as we know, employs the morality pattern to demonstrate how a student may attain knowledge. Similarly, *The Staple of News* demonstrates man's need to live with frugality if he is to achieve respect and happiness. Like some of the interludes, fourteen of the Renaissance comedies are concerned with the private affairs of a particular mankind figure. But like the political interludes, three plays, *A Looking Glasse for London and England*, *Histrio-mastix*, and *If This Be Not a Good Play*, are concerned with the welfare of an entire society.

The plays considered morality-patterned comedies depend upon the morality structure for their organization. All portray the mankind figure's life in sin, repentance, and his forgiveness. Of the seventeen plays examined, only five, *Histrio-mastix*, *The Faire Maide*, *The Dutch Curtezan*, *The Miseries of Enforced Marriage*, and *If This Be Not a Good Play*, begin with the mankind figure in a state of virtue and show his temptation and fall into sin. The remaining works begin with him in the midst of his life in sin. In these five and in all others except *If This Be Not a Good Play*, the introduction of the Vices at the beginning of the work is omitted; it is also omitted in so many Tudor interludes that one need not consider it an essential element.

Twelve plays eliminate or vary at least one of the structural elements isolated in the morality and the interlude. The temptation to despair is eliminated in six plays: *Histrio-mastix*, *All's Well That Ends Well*, *The Wise-Woman of Hogsdon*, The Second Part of *The Honest Whore*, *Match Me in London*, and *The Lady of Pleasure*. Faith that fallen man may be forgiven exists in every play, for all mankind figures are contrite and confess their crimes. In eight plays, however, they do no penance: *Misogonus*, *Histrio-mastix*, The Second Part of *The Honest Whore*, *The Miseries of Enforced Marriage*, *If This Be Not a Good Play*, *Match Me in London*, and *The Lady of Pleasure*. Both *The London Prodigal* and *The Miseries of Enforced Marriage* vary the point of repentance. The Second Part of *The Honest Whore* contracts severely the entire section dealing with the repentance of the mankind figure. Despite these variations, and as do the moralities and the interludes, these plays conclude with the mankind figure forgiven his crimes.

At the end of each work, the mankind figure is restored to his proper position in society. He suffers no loss for his life in sin, and sometimes he ends more prosperous than he began. As in the interludes, the regeneration and forgiveness of the mankind figure are expressed in terms of man's earthly life. The regenerate man becomes a responsible citizen who fulfills his social and Christian duties: the king is a magnificent ruler and a pattern of virtue for his subjects to follow; the prodigal is a liberal man; and the adulterer is a faithful husband. The mankind figures end as happy and virtuous men.

The problem of mankind's spiritual vision is central to the development of the structure. Mankind is tempted and falls because he does not recognize the Vices for the forces of evil which they are. Except in *The Miseries of Enforced Marriage*, the mankind figure is blind during his life in sin to the true nature of those who surround him. He believes, for example, that a courtesan will bring him more joy than a chaste wife. His vision must be corrected before he can repent. His recognition of his sins may tempt him at first to despair, but he always avoids such despair, because he has faith that he will receive the forgiveness of those he has wronged. After his spiritual vision is corrected, he repents, and, as he had anticipated, he is invariably forgiven.

In general, these plays employ the character types isolated in the morality and the interludes. The central character is always the mankind figure. He represents typical Christian man, torn between his spiritual and sensual natures, desiring good but tempted by evil. He always falls, he always repents, and he always receives mercy. Fifteen plays employ a single mankind figure. But as do some of the political interludes examined earlier, *A Looking Glasse for London and England* and *Histrio-mastix*, both of which are concerned with the welfare of the state, employ several. In *A Looking Glasse*, *Match Me in London*, and *If This Be Not a Good Play*, the mankind figures are kings. In *Histrio-mastix*, *All's Well*, and *The Lady of Pleasure* they are nobles. *A Looking Glasse* and *Histrio-mastix* include some mankind figures of less than noble rank. In the remaining plays, the mankind figures are middle-class citizens. Except for the First Part of *The Honest Whore* and *The Lady of Pleasure*, the mankind figures are men. All are adults and many are young. In general, the predominant sin to which a mankind figure succumbs is either lust or prodigality.

The vice figures are those characters who tempt mankind and encourage his sinfulness. Usually, they are of major importance. But in five plays, *A Looking Glasse*, *The Wise-Woman*, *The London Prodigal*, the Second Part of *The Honest Whore*, and *The Staple of News*, the vice figure is either a minor character or is omitted entirely and the vices that the mankind figure has embraced are revealed through his actions. In *The Miseries of Enforced Marriage*, the function of the vice, like that of the virtue figure, is served by Scarborow's guardian.

Excluding *The Miseries of Enforced Marriage*, which is a special case, the virtue figure in these comedies is always a major character, who helps the mankind figure turn from his life of sin. He may do so in any number of ways. Helena in *All's Well* hinders Bertram from fulfilling his sinful desires; Hippolito in the First Part of *The Honest Whore* describes eloquently the evils of Bellafront's profession; and Chrisoganus in *Histrio-mastix* indicates to the lords the path of virtue they should follow. Often, the virtue figure hears the mankind figure's confession, and, frequently, he forgives him his sins.

In conclusion, then, we can say that, in varying degrees, these plays reflect the didactic intention, action, structure, and character types that have been isolated in the morality play as it developed in the Tudor moral interlude.

Yet, clearly, they are not moralities. And they differ from the early moralities and the Tudor moral interludes in four ways. First, while some plays use allegorical figures, no play is a dramatized allegory. Second, as the discussions of the plays have illustrated, both the didactic intention and the spiritual conflict are sometimes implicit rather than explicit. Third, morality-patterned comedies include characters which do not fit into the traditional morality groupings. These may be the fools beguiled by the Vice or the mankind figure, added to provide humor or to increase the intrigue; They may be friends or relatives of the mankind figure, added to increase the play's illusion of reality or to provide information about the central characters. In short, the morality structure and the morality elements provide the playwright with a pattern that he can use as he wishes rather than with a prescription that he must follow.

Fourth and most important, these plays separate action and plot, a separation which has already begun in the Tudor moral interludes. As the terms have been defined in earlier chapters, action is the essential conflict which a play dramatizes. Plot is the unique handling of a story, through which the action is particularized and made concrete. *The Faire Maide of Bristow* will illustrate. The action is two fold: the conflict between the Virtues and the Vices for the possession of mankind's soul and the conflict between those who encourage the mankind figure to ignore his social responsibilities and those who encourage him to fulfill them. The plot deals with Vallenger's wooing and wedding of Annabell, his lust for the courtesan Florence, his intended crimes, his trial, the remission of his sentence, and his reunion with his wife. The morality-patterned comedies, therefore, can be said to develop fully the tendency toward particularization found in the Tudor moral interlude. And while only *The Miseries of Enforced Marriage* attacks a social convention, each morality-patterned comedy deals with a social problem of contemporary relevance, be it the welfare of a state or the problem of an erring husband, which it examines and always resolves on the basis of traditional Renaissance standards of proper social conduct.

These plays, therefore, "hold the mirror up to nature" and put the action in a realistic frame, so that the setting and the time are no longer as vague as possible. Usually, the play is set within a particular city, frequently London. The characters are shown in situations with which the audience would be familiar. The wives in *Histrio-mastix*, for instance, are seen buying material from a peddler; Matthew Flowerdale, the London prodigal, is shown begging; and Pennyboy, Junior, of *The Staple of News*, takes his fiancée to dinner in a London tavern. The mankind figures, moreover, are provided with their own peculiar history. We know, for example, that Misogonus' mother died a week after he was born and that his father spoiled him because the boy reminded him of his dead wife. We know that Scarborow, of *The Miseries of Enforced Marriage*, was a ward, forced to marry against his will. And we know that Vallenger is an impetuous young man who marries the belle of Bristow. The action, then, occurs in different and precise plot situations and concerns heroes who, while they are representative, are individuals as well.

Most of the plays discussed in this chapter would be accepted as comedies without any question, for most of them are clearly meant both to amuse and to instruct. Humourous plot complications and humourous characters provide obvious entertainment. The tone of most, furthermore, is unquestionably comic; that is, no matter how serious the potential outcome of the action may be, the action itself is treated with 'comic lightness' rather than with 'tragic somberness'. The description of three plays, *A Looking Glasse*, *Misogonus*, and *The Miseries of Enforced Marriage*, as comedies may, however, raise doubts since they have few of the elements which are generally associated with the comic genre. But, as will be shown, like the other plays discussed, they conform to traditional and even commonplace Renaissance theories of comedy.

The plays discussed all reveal the didactic aim traditionally associated with comedy. Sir Thomas Elyot states that comedies should be:

> ...undoubtedly a picture or as it were a mirrour of man's life, wherein iuell is nat taught but discouered; to the intent that men beholdynge the promptnes of youth unto vice, the snares of harlotts and baudes laid for yonge myndes, the disceipt of seruantes, the chaunces of fortune contrary to mennes expectation, they beinge thereof warned may prepare them selfe to resist or preuente occasion.[33]

Sir John Harington defends plays by arguing that: "The Comicall, whatsoeuer foolish playmakers make it offend in this kind, yet

---

[33] Sir Thomas Elyot, from *The Governour*, quoted in "Appendix C, Documents of Criticism", in E. K. Chambers, *The Elizabethan Stage*, IV, 187. Elyot, of course, has Latin comedy in mind, but what he writes exemplifies the English attitude toward the purpose of comedy in general.

being vsed, it represents them so as to make the vice scorned and not embraced...".³⁴ Thomas Heywood defines comedy 'according to the Latins' as "...a discourse consisting of diuers institutions, comprehending ciuill and domesticke things, in which is taught, what in our liues and manners is to be followed, what to bee auoyded".³⁵ And in "The Defence of Poesie", Sidney defines comedy as "...an imitation of the common errors of our life, which be representeth in the most ridiculous & scornfull sort that may be: so as it is impossible that any beholder can be content to be such a one."³⁶ The audiences of the morality-patterned comedies certainly learned the people and the occasions to avoid. For they learned that the riotous, the prodigals, and the lecherous bring destruction to themselves and to those who follow them. They learned that misery and ruin are the fruits of folly. They learned, finally, that only virtuous men are proper companions and that only virtuous living can bring earthly joy.

Except for those in *A Looking Glasse, If This Be Not a Good Play, Match Me in London*, and *All's Well That Ends Well*, the characters in the plays discussed are those appropriate to comedy rather than to tragedy, for they are all middle-class citizens. Excluding the political plays, *A Looking Glasse, If This Be Not a Good Play*, and *Histrio-mastix*, the works are concerned with 'private and domesticall matters' which are matters that properly belong to the comic genre.³⁷

Most important for this study, however, is the fact that all the Renaissance plays discussed which employ the morality structure must be considered comic. As Heywood's *Apology* tells us:

Tragedies and Comedies, saith Donatus, had their beginning *a rebus divinit*, from diuine sacrifices, they differ thus: In Comedies, *turbulenta*

---

[34] Sir John Harington, from *A Preface, or rather a Briefe Apologie of Poetrie, and of the Author and Translator*, quoted in "Appendix C", p. 237.

[35] Thomas Heywood, *An Apology for Actors* (1612), edited by Richard H. Perkinson (New York, Scholars' Facsimiles & Reprints, 1941), p. [F1].

[36] Sir Philip Sidney, "The Defence of Poesie", in *The Complete Works of Sir Philip Sidney*, edited by Albert Feuillerat (Cambridge, The University Press, 1923), III, 23.

[37] See, for example, Sidney's comments, *ibid*. Marvin T. Herrick has a worthwhile discussion of "The Function of Comedy" in his *Comic Theory in the Sixteenth Century* ("Illinois Studies in Language and Literature", Vol. XXIV, Nos. 1-2; Urbana, The University of Illinois Press, 1950), pp. 36-88.

*prima, tranquilla ultima,* In Tragedyes, *tranquilla prima, turbulenta ultima,* Comedies begin in trouble, and end in peace; Tragedies begin in calmes, and end in tempest.[38]

The plays which begin with the mankind figure in the midst of his life in sin clearly follow the comic movement, for they begin in turbulence and end in tranquility. In those plays in which the mankind figure begins in a state of virtue, the movement is still basically a comic one, for tempests soon come, and the action always ends in calm. It must be admitted, however, that in *The Miseries of Enforced Marriage*, the happy ending is incredibly sudden, that Scarborow and his family are saved only by gross improbability of situation and timing. This happy ending, nevertheless, cannot be ignored, since it turns a potential domestic tragedy into a morality-patterned comedy. All morality-patterned comedies end happily, and the forgiveness of the mankind figure means his restoration to an appropriate place in society and an appropriate reputation. Usually, he returns to the position he held before his fall, but in *The Staple of News*, and *The Miseries of Enforced Marriage* the mankind figure ends, at least financially, in a better position than he began. In all these plays, then, the mankind figure suffers no loss as the result of his life is sin which his repentance does not rectify.

The morality structure determines, to a great extent, the comic movement of these plays. It requires that a play move from turbulence to tranquility, for the mankind figure must fall, must repent, and must be forgiven. The conclusion, furthermore, must be merciful rather than just. No matter what sins he has committed, the mankind figure is always forgiven. Scarborow's prodigality, for example, results in poverty and pain for his wife, children, brother, and sister. Yet once he repents and is able to make restitution, his family forgives him the suffering he has caused and, indeed, seems to forget it completely. Finally, the plot must be manipulated so that the merciful conclusion is possible. In these plays, repentance brings rewards in this world. The mankind figure, therefore, cannot commit crimes which require that he receive human justice rather than human mercy. If he were, for instance, to commit murder, despite his repentance, he would have to pay

[38] Heywood, p. [F1].

for his sin with his life. Consequently, except in *A Looking Glasse*, where all is forgiven by God in a general pardon, no mankind figure commits murder. Usually, in fact, the crimes of the mankind figure are intended rather than achieved. He can, after all, be more easily forgiven what he wanted to do rather than what he has done. But plot complication does frequently arise out of this need for a merciful conclusion. In *The Wise-Woman*, *The Faire Maide*, and *The Dutch Curtezan*, to recall only three plays, much of the action results from the efforts of a virtue figure to frustrate the criminal intentions of the mankind figure. Ultimately, of course, the didactic function of the morality is responsible for the structure and the comic movement of the plays. For if the members of the audience are to be encouraged to turn from sin, they must be assured by the dramatic action that repentance will lead to forgiveness and that a life of virtue will lead to earthly happiness and probable spiritual salvation.

## CONCLUSION

The origin of this study was the hypothesis that certain Renaissance comedies could not be placed within traditional categories. An examination of the plays led to the conclusion that they could be described best by their didactic intention and their formal elements. These, it was argued, were derived ultimately from the English morality play. The result of this study, then, has been to suggest that another category of Renaissance comedy exists, one which is based upon the morality pattern. Although the 'morality-patterned comedies' are not numerous, I believe the group is large enough and vital enough to warrant attention.

As this study has sought to demonstrate, the contribution of the morality play to Renaissance comedy is greater than many scholars have supposed. It is certainly likely that the morality influenced the development of farce and probably contributed to the development of comic characters. But, in addition, it offered the playwright a pattern for comic organization. The end of the morality is to bring men back to virtuous living by assuring them that if they break with vice, repent their sins, and embrace virtue, they will be forgiven. The movement of the morality, therefore, is innately comic, because the structure has to lead to the merciful conclusion through which the didactic intention is realized. Consequently, in the morality play, the dramatist had readily available formal elements he could borrow for the development of a comic plot. Since the morality pattern was popular with audiences of the sixteenth and the early seventeenth centuries, a dramatist could use it with the knowledge that it would probably lead to a financially successful play. In short, the morality contributed to Renaissance comedy formal elements upon which the playwright could draw and a pattern upon which he could depend.

APPENDIX

## THE RELATIONSHIP BETWEEN THE MORALITY-PATTERNED COMEDY AND ENGLISH 'EDUCATION DRAMA'

*Misogonus* is commonly, and justly, held to be an example of 'education drama' written in English. Its inclusion among the morality-patterned comedies requires, therefore, that the relationship between the morality play and 'education drama' be examined. The task, fortunately, is a limited one, since only four plays are generally considered to be English 'education dramas': *A Preaty Interlude Called, Nice Wanton* (1547–1553), *The Disobedient Child* (c. 1559–1570) by Thomas Ingelend, *Misogonus* (c. 1560–1577) and *The Glasse of Government* (1575) by George Gascoigne.[1]

The classification of *Misogonus* as a morality-patterned comedy will be justified by illustrating that there is no necessary incompatability between 'education drama' and the morality play. As Palsgrave's 1540 translation of *Acolastus* demonstrates, an 'education drama' which follows the traditional development found in the parable of the prodigal son may employ, as well, the morality pattern. Since Palsgrave's translation is not a literal one, it suggests, moreover, how he and the readers of his text interpreted those 'education dramas' based upon the Biblical parable. As will be argued, both Palsgrave and his readers probably considered an 'education drama' like *Acolastus* to be one type of morality play. The three remaining English 'education dramas' do not employ the traditional development of the parable, and they vary the morality elements significantly. Consequently, they cannot be

---

[1] Felix E. Schelling *(English Drama,* London, J. M. Dent & Sons, Ltd., 1914, 64–66) and R. Warwick Bond *(Early Plays from the Italian,* Oxford, The Clarendon Press, 1911, pp. cv–cix) consider these to be examples of English 'education drama'. Madeleine Doran *(Endeavors of Art,* Madison, The University of Wisconsin Press, 1963, p. 162) omits *Glasse of Government.*

included among the morality-patterned works we have been examining.²

A few comments about the history and the nature of 'education drama' should provide an adequate foundation for the discussion to come. The history of 'education drama' is well established.³ Related to the Italian *sacre rappresentazioni*, it was developed chiefly by Dutch and German schoolmasters. Its purpose was to inculcate "...sound morality, industry, and obedience to parents and teachers", to make

> ...boys acquainted with the forms, language, and metres of Latin comedy, without the accompaniment of pagan immorality; without, that is, inviting sympathy for lying, for the deceit of and theft from fathers, without condoning or bringing to successful issue the surrender of young men to youthful temptations, or the formation of marriage connections which a parent cannot approve.⁴

Its aim, then, was to present a 'Christian Terence'.⁵ Although the plays did not imitate Terence slavishly,⁶ they derived a good many formal elements from Terentian comedy. 'Education dramas' may include, for instance, tavern and brothel scenes; and they may make use of the contrast between severe and indulgent parents, virtuous and riotous sons, or faithful and unprincipled servants — all typical of New Comedy.⁷ Some begin in the Terentian manner, with a father discussing his son's recklessness with a friend. Finally, 'education dramas' may be set in Rome, and the names of the characters may be Latinized. The plots for 'education dramas' were usually based upon Biblical tales, most often that

---

² At times scholars have grouped morality plays or moral interludes with 'education dramas'. For example, Henry Hitch Adams considers *Nice Wanton* and *Glasse of Government* to belong with the morality plays *(English Domestic, or Homilectic Tragedy, 1575 to 1642*, "Columbia University Studies in English and Comparative Literature", No. 159; New York, Columbia University Press, 1943, pp. 67–73). Miss Doran groups *Nice Wanton* and *Glasse of Government* with *Mundus & Infans* and *Lusty Juventus*, all of which she considers to be Prodigal Son plays (p. 142).

³ The discussions of R. Warwick Bond (pp. xci–cix) and Marvin T. Herrick ("Chapter Two. Contribution of the Christian Terence to Tragicomedy", *Tragicomedy*, "Illinois Studies in Language and Literature". No. 39; Urbana, The University of Illinois Press, 1955, pp. 16–62) are the best on this subject.

⁴ Bond, p. xciii.
⁵ *Ibid.*
⁶ Herrick, p. 61.
⁷ Bond, p. xciii.

of the prodigal son. The parable, however, could be adapted, as it was in Macropedius' *Rebelles*, to present "...a reproduction of contemporary school-life".[8] All have a strong didactic purpose. They teach, for example, that the indulgent parent brings unhappiness to himself and to his children; that obedience, piety, and sobriety will bring man earthly rewards; that disobedience, irreligion, and prodigality will bring him to disaster.

Of the plays to be discussed here, *Acolastus* is the only one which can be properly called 'education drama', as the term has been defined above. For it is the only one written in Latin and meant to be used as a teaching device. Palsgrave's translation was prepared, of course, as a teaching aid. Obviously, the four 'education dramas' written in English do not have such a purpose. But they reflect the influence of Latin 'education dramas', and they are their English counterparts.

*Acolastus* was written by the Dutchman Wilhelm de Volder (also known as Gnaphaues or Fullonius) in 1528 and translated from Latin into English by John Palsgrave in 1540. As we learn from the Prologue, the play is a purposeful fusion of the parable of the prodigal son and Latin comedy.[9] Its plot and the two major characters are based upon the parable, while many of the other elements, including the opening, the gambling scenes, and the minor characters, are derived from New Comedy. Nevertheless, as we shall see, *Acolastus* employs the morality pattern as well.

The play opens in the Terentian manner.[10] Pelargus consults with his friend Eubulus about Acolastus, Pelargus' son. From this discussion, the audience learns that Acolastus is a willful boy who insists upon receiving his portion so that he can leave home and, thus, be free to pursue sensual pleasures. As the remainder of the play illustrates, Eubulus counsels his friend wisely when he suggests that, if Acolastus cannot be convinced by reason to stay, Pelargus should let him go as he desires; for, undoubtedly, Acolastus will

[8] *Ibid.* p. xcix.

[9] John Palsgrave, *The Comedy of Acolastus, translated from the Latin of Fullonius, by John Palsgrave*, edited by P. L. Carver ("Early English Text Society". No. CCII; London, Humphrey Milford, Oxford University Press, 1937), pp. 15–21. Other references to the play will be made in the body of the text.

[10] For example, *The Self-Tormentor (Heauton Timorumenos)* begins in a similar manner.

soon perceive the error of his decision and will then return home a wiser and more obedient son.

In the following scene, Acolastus appears and reveals himself to be in the midst of a life in sin. His fallen state is indicated by his friendship with Philautus, who advises him "...to dysobey his father, & to lyue after his sensual apetite" (p. 13), and who, later, convinces the youth to discard the Bible Pelargus had given him as a farewell gift. Acolastus receives his portion and travels to another country. Prodigal, he wastes his fortune in gambling and in lavish entertainment. Lustful, he woos the courtesan Lais. His pursuit of sensual pleasures and his evil companions finally bring him to financial ruin. Once his wealth is gone, those he had entertained desert him. As in the parable, there is a famine in the land, and the prodigal is forced to support himself by feeding swine.

Through his misery, his spiritual vision is corrected. He finally recognizes the evil nature of his companions and regrets his past follies: "...on whom may I laye the wyte or the faute, or to whom may I impute this myschance (of myne?) vnto theym, whiche haue entyced me to to deceyfully into these perils... or to me, which haue harkned (to them)... or to myne angry *Genius*". (pp. 148-49) He is tempted to despair and contemplates suicide: "...wolde to god it myght be leful for me to breake this lyghte behated. i. to fordoo my selfe, or to make an ende of me, or to kyll my selfe, rather that I shulde trayle or lynger my lyfe in so many and so great infelycites". (p. 161) Instead, shortly afterwards, he decides to go to his father and ask his forgiveness. For, miraculously, Acolastus has been given hope of mercy: "...beholde this thyng is sodynly breathed vnto me... that my father is good, easy to be appesed or pleased, and deuout or tender harted, and from thens dothe hope of forgyuenes shyne towards me..." (p. 173). Contrite, he approaches his father, confessing: "Father, I haue synned into the heuen, and before the, nor here after I am not worthy to be called thy sonne." (p. 176) While he does no penance, during the famine he has certainly suffered adequately for his sins. His father, of course, is merciful: "All thynges be forgyuen to the. i. all these offences and trespaces be forgiuen the." (p. 176) Acolastus, at the end of the play, is restored to his former honored position in his father's household. As this brief summary demonstrates, despite the elements derived from the parable and from Latin comedy, the structure of the play is similar to that of the morality, the moral interlude, and the morality-patterned comedy.

While it does not employ allegorical figures, the play does employ characters whose functions are similar to the characters in the morality. Acolastus is a mankind figure: he is tempted by sensual pleasures, falls into a life of sin, is tempted to despair, recognizes his folly, repents, and is forgiven. Pelargus, his father, is the major virtue figure, who wishes his son to lead a godly life, one guided by Biblical precepts. As do the mercy characters in the older moralities, he listens to his son's repentance and forgives him his sins. Opposed to him is Philautus, Acolastus' evil counsellor, who functions as the major vice figure. He and Pelargus are, as he himself tells us, "...mortally enmyes togyther". (p. 46) By encouraging Acolastus to seek sensual satisfaction, he tempts him to follow a way of life which is socially condemned and which threatens his spiritual well-being. Philautus clearly reveals himself to be one of the Devil's party when he persuades Acolastus to discard the Bible his father has given him because "there is noo boke more enemy vnto us than this is..." (p. 58).

The action, furthermore, is the same as that found in the morality. For it concerns the struggle between the Vices and the Virtues for the possession of mankind's soul. By following the counsels of Philautus, Acolastus not only brings about his financial ruin, but he threatens the salvation of his soul as well, since he commits sins which would certainly lead to spiritual damnation if he did not repent. By following the counsels of his father, on the other hand, he lives virtuously and so works toward salvation.

Finally, the didactic intention of *Acolastus* is exactly like that of the morality. As the Perroration states, from the play one learns: "howe iustly mankyned through his resystyn or styffenes of harte, hath deseured to dye euerlastyngly. But on the contrary syde, thou haste .i. thou mayste here perceyue, how great the tendernes of goddis benignities or mercyfulnesse is". (p. 180) In the work, then, man learns that for his spiritual well-being he must avoid vice and embrace virtue and that, if he repents, he will be forgiven.

The similarity of the play to the morality should not surprise us. We know that the morality form was known in Holland and that *Everyman* is probably of Dutch origin. It is, therefore, quite possible that Volder used morality elements to develop the plot.

The parable of the prodigal son, moreover, follows a morality pattern, beginning with mankind's life in sin and ending with his forgiveness and his restoration to his proper place. The parable even suggests the didactic intention of the morality, since the son is meant to be sinful man and the father to be God.

Without doubt, Palsgrave, and presumably the readers of his text, considered *Acolastus* to be a dramatization of the relationship between man and God. Palsgrave translates:

> *Quippe, perdito salus*
> *Vt parta sit homini, reteximus, uelut*
> *Imagine oculis prodita.*

as follows:

> For why, we haue unweaued .i. discouered and made open (vnto you) howe helthe hath bene gotten to the loste man .i. *howe mankynde, whiche was vndone, or cast awaye, hath recouered his saluation agayne*, as by an ymage bewrayed to the eyes... (p. 179, italics mine)

The italicized lines are of particular interest to this study because the terminology is the same as that used in the morality. They suggest, therefore, that Palsgrave, and probably the readers of his text, considered *Acolastus* and any other prodigal son plays employing the same elements and structure to be one type of morality play.[11]

Of the four plays considered to be 'education dramas' written in English, *Misogonus* is the only one that can be compared with *Acolastus*.[12] As does the Latin play, it retains the general plot development of the parable, while it depends heavily upon the morality for its didactic intention and most of its formal elements. The remaining English 'education dramas' differ from these works because they alter the formal elements of the morality drastically.

*A Preaty Interlude Called, Nice Wanton* (1547–1553)[13] demonstra-

---

[11] In this regard, it is interesting to recall that in *Eastward Ho*, Touchstone calls the play 'a morall': "And in this morall, see thy Glasse runne out" (*Eastward Ho*, in *Ben Jonson*, edited by C. H. Herford and Percy Simpson, IV, Oxford, The Clarendon Press, 1932, V, v, 206).

[12] See Chapter IV, p. 105.

[13] Miss Doran considers *Nice Wanton* and *The Disobedient Child* to be good examples of the prodigal type story placed in 'the abstract frame of the moral play' (p. 162). As my discussion will show, I do not agree.

tes that the spoiled child brings ruin to himself and shame to his family. The interlude traces the history of three siblings: Ismael and Dalila, the spoiled children of Xantipe, and Barnabas, her diligent and virtuous son. The former refuse to go to school, preferring to spend their days in idleness and sensual pursuits. Their counsellor and companion is the Vice Iniquitie. Because of their wantonness, both come to ruin: Ismael is executed for theft and murder; Dalila becomes a prostitute and dies of the pox.

The interlude is concerned primarily with the evil effects of maternal indulgence. As the Prologue tells the audience:

> The prudent prince, Salomon, doth say
> 'He that spareth the rod, the chyld doth hate';[14]

for

> If chyldren be noseled in idlenes and yll
> And brought vp therein, it is hard to restrayne
> And draw them from naturall wont euyll,
> As here in thys interlude ye shall see playne. (ll. 9-12)

As in other 'education dramas', therefore, the indulgent parent is considered to be responsible for the wantonness of the child.

Many morality elements are present. Ismael and Dalila begin in the midst of their lives in sin, indicated by their refusal to attend school and developed through a scene in which they are shown gambling with Iniquitie. Xantipe, too, might be considered in the midst of her life in sin; for despite the counsel of Eulalia, her neighbor and a virtuous mother, she does not recognize the wantonness of her children, and she refuses to punish them. Eventually, all three recognize their follies. Dalila realizes that her poverty and ill health are deserved: "Iustly for my sinnes God doth plague me". (l. 276) Just before his execution, Ismael perceives that Iniquitie has been an evil influence. Both Dalila and Xantipe are tempted to despair. The daughter fears that because of her sins, she is "...to be damned for-euermore". (l. 284) Worldly Shame

---

[14] *A Preaty Interlude Called, Nice Wanton*, in *Specimens of the Pre-Shakespearean Drama*, edited by John Matthews Manly, I (Boston, Ginn and Company, 1897), ll. 1-2. Other references to the play will be made in the body of the text.

informs the mother of the deaths of her children and accuses her of being the cause. As a result, she attempts to commit suicide but is stopped by Barnabas, who tells her that both Ismael and Dalila repented before their deaths and persuades her to do so as well.

The characters reflect the morality types. The wanton children and Xantipe function as mankind figures, who may sin, but who are capable of repentance. Iniquitie and Wordlly Shame are Vices. The former tempts the children into a life of sin by encouraging Ismael's prodigality and Dalila's lust. The latter tries to bring about Xantipe's suicide and so her spiritual damnation. Barnabas functions as a virtue figure. When a youth, he tries to shame his brother and his sister into abandoning their sensual pursuits and living virtuously. Having found Dalila ill and impoverished as a result of her life in sin, he helps her and encourages her to repent. He stops his mother from committing suicide and urges her not to despair because, if she, too, repents, "...God will frely remitte your sinnes all". (l. 518)

The play reflects the struggle between the Vices and the Virtues for the possession of mankind's soul, which forms the action of a morality play. Barnabas attempts unsuccessfully to draw the young Dalila and Ismael away from the evil influence of Iniquitie. At last, he succeeds in defeating both Iniquitie and Worldly Shame by contributing to the regeneration of the members of his family.

*Nice Wanton*, moreover, suggests the didactic intention found in the morality. It indicates that sinful man, if he repents, has hope of divine mercy. Speaking to his mother, Barnabas implies that Dalila will be forgiven her sins:

> Before her death she beleued that God, of his mercy,
> For Christes sake, would saue her eternally. (ll. 515-16)

And he assures Xantipe that if she repents, God will remit her sins, because, "Christe hath payed the raunsom". (l. 519)

Despite the fact that *Nice Wanton* contains numerous morality elements, it cannot be considered either a traditional moral interlude or a morality-patterned comedy. It does not belong with the interludes discussed earlier because it attempts realistic characterization. More important, however, it differs from the moral interlude and the morality-patterned comedy in three significant ways. First, repentance is not part of the dramatic structure, as it is in all such works. Second, while forgiveness of the mankind figures is hoped for and even anticipated, it is not part of the play's dramatic structure, as it is in all interludes and morality-patterned comedies. Third, the comic movement of the morality structure has been altered. As was pointed out in Chapter IV, this movement affects the plot. Forgiveness of the sins committed by the mankind figure is the final structural element of all moralities, moral interludes, and morality-patterned comedies. In those plays attempting realism — that is, the morality-patterned comedies — it is always expressed in terms of man's earthly life. The mankind figures, as a result, do not commit crimes which would require human justice rather than human mercy, and they never die. In *Nice Wanton*, however, Ismael is executed for theft and murder, and Dalila dies of the pox. The mercy they hope to receive will be in the next world, not in this. Consequently, if forgiveness is assumed, the play has a double ending. It ends sadly because both die for their sins, and it ends happily because they have achieved their spiritual salvation. No such double ending exists in the moralities, the moral interludes, or the morality-patterned comedies. When the ways of the world and the ways of God are separated, the problem of mercy in this world does not arise. When they are fused, spiritual forgiveness is indicated by the restoration of the mankind figure to his proper worldly position and reputation. For these reasons, *Nice Wanton* cannot be grouped with the morality plays discussed here.

Thomas Ingelend's *The Disobedient Child* (1559–1570) deals with the results of disobedience and prodigality. The Young Man has been spoiled by his father, the Rich Man. As a result, he refuses to follow his father's counsel and will neither study nor work. Despite his father's opposition, he decides to marry, and he plans to live a slothful and sensual life. His father, consequently, disowns him. The Young Man borrows money, marries, and for a short time lives extravagantly and happily with his bride. Soon, however, as his father had predicted, the son becomes impoverished, and his wife becomes a shrew. In order to support himself and his wife, the husband gathers faggots. In a monologue, the Devil tells the audience that he is the cause of the Young Man's misery; for it was he who tempted him to disobey his father. Regretting his willfulness and disobedience, the Young Man seeks his father's forgiveness. But despite his love for his son, the Rich Man offers him only temporary relief and tells him, "I am not he that will thee retain".[15]

*The Disobedient Child* has the same didactic intentions as those found in Latin 'education dramas'. As the Perorator states, the play is meant to teach the father:

> After what manner his child to use,
> Lest that through cockering at length he be brought
> His father's commandment to refuse (p. 316),

and it is meant to teach the child:

> By your loving parents always be ruled,
> Or else be well assured of such a fall,
> As unto this young man worthily chanced.
> Worship God daily, which is the chief thing,
> And his holy laws do not offend:
> Look that ye truly serve the king,
> Moreover, be true of hand and tongue,
> And learn to do all things that be honest. (p. 318)

Here, then, are reflected typical concerns of 'education drama': the evil effects of parental indulgence, and the ruin brought by disobedience, slothfulness, and prodigality.

The play exhibits few traditional morality elements. The first scene, in which the Rich Man tries to dissuade his son from marrying, is reminiscent of those in the morality between the virtue figure and mankind. The Young Man is certainly in the midst of his life in sin and blinded by his sensual desires. As does a mankind figure, he finally recognizes his folly and regrets his actions. Contrite, he confesses his sins:

> The thing that was good I greatly hated,
> As one which lacked both wit and reason;
> The thing that was evil I ever loved,
> Which now I see is my confusion. (p. 312)

---

[15] Thomas Ingelend, *The Disobedient Child*, in *A Select Collection of Old English Plays*, edited by W. Carew Hazlitt (4th ed.; London, Reeves and Turner, 1874), II, 316. Other references to the play will be made in the body of the text.

Two other characters recall traditional morality types. Satan, of course, is a force of evil, and the Rich Man, since he does try to guide his son to virtue, is similar to a force of good. On the whole, however, *The Disobedient Child* differs significantly from the morality pattern we are investigating. The structure is altered drastically, for the Young Man's repentance is not accepted by his father, and he is not forgiven. Consequently, instead of receiving mercy for his sins, he receives justice only. Although Satan says that he has brought about the Young Man's ruin, he has no such function in the play. The Rich Man, moreover, is an inadequate virtue figure, both because, by having spoiled the boy, he is ultimately responsible for his son's willful behavior and because he refuses to be merciful to a repentant sinner. The action differs as well, for there is no conflict between the Vices and the Virtues for the possession of mankind's soul. Despite the presence of Satan, the problem of spiritual salvation does not even appear in the play. The Young Man has, indeed, brought himself to financial ruin and misery, but he has not, as a result, brought about his spiritual damnation, for he has recognized and repented the sins he has committed. Finally, unlike the morality, the play does not teach the audience that sinful man, if he repents, has hope of mercy and salvation. Instead, it points out that the spoiled and disobedient child will bring unhappiness to himself and to his parents.

Although Gascoigne's *The Glasse of Government* (1575) has been considered by some scholars to be a translation of a morality,[16] the play contains very few morality elements. Its purpose is to demonstrate the rewards of virtue and the fruits of vice. The play contrasts reckless older sons and sober younger ones, all of whom

---

[16] Thomas W. Baldwin believes the play is "...a translation of some morality which he had procured in Holland when he was there in 1573-4" *(Shakspere's Five-Act Structure*, Urbana, University of Illinois Press, 1947, p. 451). A. Bronson Feldman agrees that the work is a translation but thinks the original was probably French, "...the work of a Catholic dramatist of Brabont, not long after 1562, when Douai University ('lately erected') opened its doors" ("Dutch Humanism and the Tudor Dramatic Tradition", *Notes and Queries*, 197, August 16, 1952, p. 360). There is some doubt as to whether or not the play was ever performed. Bond feels it may not have been intended for performance (p. cvii); E. K. Chambers believes it may have been a closet drama *(The Elizabethan Stage*, Oxford, The Clarendon Press, 1923, III, 321).

are taught by the virtuous schoolmaster, Gnomaticus. The older are the quicker students and, at first, seem to have the greater promise. But their downfall is indicated early in the play by their refusal to treat seriously the Christian teachings of Gnomaticus. The younger children become the better students, for, though they are slower, they study harder and so learn more. Eventually, the older sons, tempted by the parasite Echho and abetted by the servant Ambidexter, give themselves completely to sensual satisfactions and surround themselves with evil companions such as Lamia, a prostitute, and Dick Droom, a wastral. Their sins soon bring about their ruin: one is executed at the Palsgrave court for robbery; the other is whipped and banished from Geneva because of fornication. The virtuous sons, on the other hand, win the reputation and success they deserve: one becomes a secretary to the Palsgrave court; the other becomes a famous preacher in Geneva.

The play has a good deal in common with Latin 'education drama', for its didactic purpose is to show "...the rewardes and punishmentes of vertues and vices".[17] And it stresses the importance of obedience to God, state, teacher, and parent. The virtues it commends are those with which 'education drama' is particularly concerned: sobriety, industriousness, and studiousness. Although in the Prologue, Gascoigne attacks Terentian comedy, "No Terence phrase: his tyme and myne are twaine" (p. 6), its influence is evident in the play. For while the setting is Antwerp, the names of the characters are Latinized; the virtuous sons are contrasted with the reckless sons; and the virtuous servant, Fidus, is contrasted with the crafty and evil servant, Ambidexter.

The morality elements, however, are minor. As does the older morality, *Glasse* begins and ends with a statement of moral purpose. The temptation and fall of the older sons are shown, and their evil companions are reminiscent of the Vices in the morality. Gnomaticus functions as a virtue figure when he tries to teach the boys to avoid vice, attempts to turn the older brothers toward virtue, and comments upon the moral significance of the plot.

---

[17] George Gascoigne, *The Glasse of Government*, in *The Complete Works of George Gascoigne*, edited by John W. Cunliffe (Cambridge, The University Press, 1910), II, 5. Other references to the play will be made in the body of the text.

The difference between *Glasse of Government* and the morality is, nevertheless, profound. In Gascoigne's work, the problem of spiritual salvation is not really raised, for the play is concerned with illustrating the earthly rewards the virtuous obtain and the earthly punishments the vicious receive. In addition, the play rejects the premise upon which the didactic intention and the formal elements of the morality depend, the premise that sinful man is capable of regeneration. As the Fourth Chorus states:

> ... all too late the water comes, when house is burned quite.
> Wherefore who list to learne: *Obsta Principiis*.
> Since vertue seldome can prevaile, where vice so rooted is. (p. 71)

*Glasse of Government*, consequently, has little in common with morality-patterned works.

Studies of *Acolastus* and the four 'education dramas' written in English bring two conclusions. First, the prodigal son play, when it follows the traditional movement of the parable from sin to repentance, is similar in pattern to the morality. *Misogonus* is the only English example. Second, the other English 'education dramas' differ significantly from the morality plays, the moral interludes, and the morality-patterned comedies with which this work is concerned. In *The Disobedient Child* and *The Glasse of Government*, the struggle for spiritual salvation does not arise, and in *Nice Wanton* it is subordinated to the problem of maternal indulgence. In all three, the ending is unhappy, for the sinners have been brought to ruin or have died because of their sins. Most important, in all but *Misogonus*, the sinner receives justice rather than mercy for his sins. Of the English 'education dramas', therefore, only *Misogonus* can be described accurately as a morality-patterned work.

# BIBLIOGRAPHY

## PRIMARY SOURCES

### Plays

Bale, John, *A Comedy Concerning Three Laws, of Nature, Moses, and Christ*, in *The Dramatic Writings of John Bale*, edited by John S. Farmer (London, Early English Drama Society, 1907).
—, *A Comedy or Interlude Concerning the Temptation of our Lord and Saviour Jesus Christ by Satan*, in *The Dramatic Writings of John Bale*, edited by John S. Farmer (London, Early English Drama Society, 1907).
—, *A Tragedy of John, King of England*, in *The Dramatic Writings of John Bale*, edited by John S. Farmer (London, Early English Drama Society, 1907).
—, *A Tragedy or Interlude Manifesting the Chief Promises of God unto Man*, in *The Dramatic Writings of John Bale*, edited by John S. Farmer (London, Early English Drama Society, 1907).
Beaumont, Francis and Fletcher, John, *A King and No King*, in *The Works of Francis Beaumont and John Fletcher*, edited by Arnold Glover, Vol. I (Cambridge, The University Press, 1905).
*The Castell of Perseverance*, in *The Macro Plays*, edited by F. J. Furnivall and Alfred W. Pollard, "Early English Text Society", Extra Series XCI (London, Kegan Paul, Trench, Trubner & Co., 1904).
Chapman, George, *All Fooles*, in *The Comedies and Tragedies of George Chapman, Now First Collected with Illustrative Notes, and a Memoir of the Author in Three Volumes* [Edited by Richard Herne Shepherd] Vol. I (London, John Pearson, 1873).
*The Contention Between Liberality and Prodigality*, edited by W. W. Greg, "The Malone Society Reprints", Vol. 1913-A (Cambridge, Oxford University Press, 1913).
*A Contract of Marriage Between Wit and Wisdom*, supervised and edited by John S. Farmer, "The Tudor Facsimile Texts" [Vol. XLIII.] (London and Edinburgh, T. C. & E. C. Jack, 1909).
Dekker, Thomas and Middleton, Thomas, *The Honest Whore, Part I*, in *The Dramatic Works of Thomas Dekker*, edited by Fredson Bowers, Vol. II (Cambridge, The University Press, 1955).

Dekker, Thomas, *The Honest Whore, Part II*, in *The Dramatic Works of Thomas Dekker*, edited by Fredson Bowers, Vol. II (Cambridge, The University Press, 1955).
—, *If This Be Not a Good Play, the Devil Is In It*, in *The Dramatic Works of Thomas Dekker*, edited by Fredson Bowers, Vol. III (Cambridge, The University Press, 1958).
—, *Match Me in London*, in *The Dramatic Works of Thomas Dekker*, edited by Fredson Bowers, Vol. III (Cambridge, The University Press, 1958).
*Everyman*, edited by A. C. Cawley (Manchester, Manchester University Press, 1961).
*The Faire Maide of Bristow*, edited by Arthur Hobson Quinn, "Publications of the University of Pennsylvania Series in Philology and Literature", Vol. VIII, No. 1 (Philadelphia, Ginn and Company, 1902).
Fulwell, Ulpian, *Like Will to Like*, in *A Select Collection of Old English Plays*, edited by W. Carew Hazlitt, Vol. III, 4th ed. (London, Reeves and Turner, 1874).
Garter, Thomas, *The Most Virtuous and Godly Susanna*, edited by B. Ifor Evans and W. W. Greg, "The Malone Society Reprints", Vol. LXXIV (Cambridge, Oxford University Press, 1937).
Gascoigne, George, *The Glasse of Government*, in *The Complete Works of George Gascoigne*, edited by John W. Cunliffe, Vol. II (Cambridge, The University Press, 1910).
—, *Supposes*, in *The Complete Works of George Gascoigne*, edited by John W. Cunliffe, Vol. I (Cambridge, The University Press, 1907).
Greene, Robert and Lodge, Thomas, *A Looking Glasse for London and England*, in *The Plays and Poems of Robert Greene*, edited by J. Churton Collins, Vol. I (Oxford, The Clarendon Press, 1905).
Heywood, Thomas, *The Wise-Woman of Hogsdon*, in *Thomas Heywood*, edited by A. Wilson Verity, "The Mermaid Series", Vol. I (London, Vizetelly and Co., 1888).
*Histrio-mastix*, in *The School of Shakespeare*, edited by Richard Simpson, Vol. II (London, Chatto and Windus, 1878).
*How a Man May Chuse a Good Wife From a Bad*, edited by A. E. H. Swaen, "Materialien zur Kunde des alteren Englischen Dramas", Vol. XXXV (Louvain, A. Uystpryst, 1912).
*Hyckescorner*, in *Specimens of the Pre-Shakespearean Drama*, edited by John Matthews Manly, Vol. I (Boston, Ginn and Company, 1897).
*Impatient Poverty*, in *Recently Recovered "Lost" Tudor Plays with Some Others*, edited by John S. Farmer (London, Early English Drama Society, 1907).
Ingelend, Thomas, *The Disobedient Child*, in *A Select Collection of Old English Plays*, edited by W. Carew Hazlitt, Vol. II, 4th ed. (London, Reeves and Turner, 1874).
*An Interlude of Wealth and Health*, in *Recently Recovered "Lost" Tudor Plays with Some Others*, edited by John S. Farmer (London, Early English Drama Society, 1907).
*The Interlude of Youth*, in *A Select Collection of Old English Plays*, edited by W. Carew Hazlitt, Vol. II, 4th ed. (London, Reeves and Turner, 1874).

Jonson, Ben, Chapman, George, and Marston, John, *Eastward Ho*, in *Ben Jonson*, edited by C. H. Herford and Percy Simpson, Vol. IV (Oxford, The Clarendon Press, 1932).

Jonson, Ben, *The Staple of News*, in *Ben Jonson*, edited by C. H. Herford and Percy Simpson, Vol. VI (Oxford, The Clarendon Press, 1932).

—, *Volpone, or the Fox*, in *Ben Jonson*, edited by C. H. Herford and Percy Simpson, Vol. V (Oxford, The Clarendon Press, 1937).

*King Darius*, in *Quellen des Weltlichen Dramas in England vor Shakespeare*, edited by Alois Brandl (Strassburg, Karl J. Trubner, 1898).

Lindsay, Sir David, *Ane Satyre of the Thrie Estaitis*, in *The Poetical Works of Sir David Lindsay*, edited by David Laing, Vol. II (Edinburgh, William Paterson, 1879).

*The London Prodigal*, in *The Doubtful Plays of William Shakespeare*, edited by William Hazlitt (London, George Routledge and Sons, 1887).

Lupton, Thomas, *All for Money*, in *Jahrbuch der Deutschen Shakespeare-Gesellschaft*, edited by Alois Brandl and Wolfgang Keller, Vol. XL (Berlin, Langenscheidtsche Verlagsbuchhandlung, 1904).

*Mankind*, in *The Macro Plays*, edited by F. J. Furnivall and Alfred W. Pollard, "Early English Text Society", Extra Series XCI (London, Kegan Paul, Trench, Trubner & Co., 1904).

*The Marriage of Wit and Science*, supervised and edited by John S. Farmer, "The Tudor Facsimile Texts", [Vol. XLII] (London and Edinburgh, T. C. & E. C. Jack, 1909).

Marston, John, *The Dutch Curtezan*, in *The Plays of John Marston*, edited by H. Harvey Wood, Vol. II (London and Edinburgh, Oliver and Boyd, 1938).

*Mary Magdalene*, in *The Digby Mysteries*, edited by F. J. Furnivall, "The Early English Text Society", Extra Series, No. LXX, Reissue (London, Kegan Paul, Trench, Trubner & Co., 1896).

*The Massacre of the Innocents*, in *Ludus Coventriae or The Plaie called Corpus Christi*, edited by K. A. Block, "The Early English Text Society", No. CXX (London, Oxford University Press, 1922).

Medwall, Henry, *Nature*, in *Recently Recovered "Lost" Tudor Plays with Some Others*, edited by John S. Farmer (London, Early English Drama Society, 1907).

*Misogonus*, in *Early Plays from the Italian*, edited by R. Warwick Bond (Oxford, The Clarendon Press, 1911).

*A Morality of Wisdom, Who is Christ*, in *The Macro Plays*, edited by F. J. Furnivall and Alfred W. Pollard, "Early English Text Society", Extra Series XCI (London, Kegan Paul, Trench, Trubner & Co., 1904).

*Mundus et Infans*, in *Specimens of the Pre-Shakespearean Drama*, edited by John Matthews Manly, Vol. I (Boston, Ginn and Company, 1897).

*A New Enterlude of Godly Queene Hester*, edited by W. W. Greg, "Materialien zur Kunde des alteren Englischen Dramas", Vol. V (Louvain, A. Uystpruyst, 1904).

Palsgrave, John, *The Comedy of Acolastus, translated from the Latin of Fullonius, by John Palsgrave*, edited by P. L. Carver, "Early English Text Society", No. CCII (London, Humphrey Milford, Oxford University Press, 1937).

Pickering, John, *The Interlude of Vice (Horestes)*, in *Quellen des Weltlichen Dramas in England vor Shakespeare*, edited by Alois Brandl (Strassburg, Karl J. Trubner, 1898).

*A Preaty Interlude Called, Nice Wanton*, in *Specimens of the Pre-Shakespearean Drama*, edited by John Matthews Manly, Vol. I (Boston, Ginn and Company, 1897).

*Pride of Life*, in *The Non-Cycle Mystery Plays, together with the Croxton Play of the Sacrament and the Pride of Life*, edited by Osborn Waterhouse, "Early English Text Society", Extra Series, No. 104 (London, Kegan Paul, Trubner & Co., 1909).

Rastell, John, *The Interlude of the Four Elements*, in *A Select Collection of Old English Plays*, edited by W. Carew Hazlitt, Vol. I, 4th ed. (London, Reeves and Turner, 1874).

Redford, John, *The Play of Wyt and Science*, in *Specimens of the Pre-Shakespearean Drama*, edited by John Matthews Manly, Vol. I (Boston, Ginn and Company, 1897).

*Respublica*, in *Recently Recovered "Lost" Tudor Plays with Some Others*, edited by John S. Farmer (London, Early English Drama Society, 1907).

*The Salutation and Conception*, in *Ludus Coventriae or The Plaie Called Corpus Christi*, edited by K. S. Block, "The Early English Text Society", No. CXX (London, Oxford University Press, 1922).

Shakespeare, William, *All's Well That Ends Well*, edited by G. K. Hunter, "The Arden Shakespeare", 3rd ed. (London, Metheun and Co., Ltd., 1959).

—, *As You Like It*, in *The Complete Works of Shakespeare*, edited by George Lyman Kittredge (Boston, Ginn and Company, 1936).

Shirley, James, *The Lady of Pleasure*, in *The Dramatic Works and Poems of James Shirley*, edited by William Gifford, Vol. IV (London, John Murray, 1833).

Skelton, John, *Magnyfycence, a Moral Play by John Skelton*, edited by Robert Lee Ramsey, "Early English Text Society", Extra Series No. XCVIII (London, Kegan Paul, Trench, Trubner and Co., Ltd., 1908).

Terence, *The Self-Tormentor*, in *Terence*, with an English Translation by John Sargeaunt, "Loeb Classical Library", Vol. I (London and New York, William Heinemann and G. P. Putnam's Sons, 1912).

Wager, Lewis, *The Life and Repentaunce of Marie Magdalene*, edited by Frederic Ives Carpenter (Chicago, The University of Chicago Press, 1904).

Wager, W., *Enough is as Good as a Feast*, introductory note by Seymour De Ricci, "The Henry E. Huntington Facsimile Reprints", Vol. II (New York, George D. Smith, 1920).

—, *The Longer Thou Livest, the More Foole Thou Art*, in *Jahrbuch der Deutschen Shakespeare-Gesellschaft*, edited by Alois Brandl and Wolfgang Keller, Vol. XXXVI (Berlin, Langenscheidtsche Verlagsbuchhandlung, 1900).

—, *The Trial of Treasure*, in *A Select Collection of Old English Plays*, edited by W. Carew Hazlitt, Vol. III, 4th ed. (London, Reeves and Turner, 1874).

Walpull, George, *The Tyde Tarrieth No Man*, in *Jahrbuch der Deutschen Shakespeare-Gesellschaft*, edited by Alois Brandl and Wolfgang Keller, Vol. XLIII (Berlin, Langenscheidtsche Verlagsbuchhandlung, 1907).

Wever, R., *Lusty Juventus*, in *A Select Collection of Old English Plays*, edited by W. Carew Hazlitt, Vol. II, 4th ed. (London, Reeves and Turner, 1874).

Wilkins, George, *The Miseries of Enforced Marriage*, in *A Select Collection of Old English Plays*, edited by W. Carew Hazlitt, Vol. IX, 4th ed. (London, Reeves and Turner, 1874).

Wilson, Robert, *The Three Ladies of London*, in *A Select Collection of Old English Plays*, edited by W. Carew Hazlitt, Vol. VI, 4th ed. (London, Reeves and Turner, 1874).

## *Others*

Elyot, Sir Thomas, Passages from *The Governour*, quoted in "Appendix C, Documents of Criticism", E. K. Chambers, *The Elizabethan Stage*, IV (Oxford, The Clarendon Press, 1923), 187.

Harington, Sir John, Passages from *A Preface, or rather a Briefe Apologie of Poetrie, and of the Author and Translator*, quoted in "Appendix C, Documents of Criticism", E. K. Chambers, *The Elizabethan Stage*, IV (Oxford, The Clarendon Press, 1923), 237–238.

Heywood, Thomas, *An Apology for Actors*, edited by Richard H. Perkinson (New York, Scholars' Facsimiles and Reprints, 1941).

Rich, Barnaby, *Rich's Farewell to Military Profession, 1581*, edited by Thomas Mabry Cranfill (Austin, University of Texas Press, 1959).

Sidney, Sir Philip, "The Defence of Poesie", in *The Complete Works of Sir Philip Sidney*, edited by Albert Feuillerat, Vol. III (Cambridge, The University Press, 1923).

## SCHOLARLY STUDIES

Adams, Henry Hitch, *English Domestic or, Homiletic Tragedy, 1575 to 1642*. "Columbia University Studies in English and Comparative Literature", No. 159 (New York, Columbia University Press, 1943).

Baldwin, Thomas W., *Shakspere's Five-Act Structure* (Urbana, University of Illinois Press, 1947).

Baskervill, C. R., "Source and Analogues of 'How a Man May Choose a Good Wife From a Bad'", *Publications of the Modern Language Association of America*, XXIV, New Series XVII (1909), 711–730.

Bates, Katharine Lee, *The English Religious Drama* (New York, The Macmillan Company, 1902).

Baum, Helena Watts, *The Satiric and the Didactic in Ben Jonson's Comedy* (Chapel Hill, The University of North Carolina Press, 1947).

Bevington, David M., *From Mankind to Marlowe* (Cambridge, Harvard University Press, 1962).

—, "Political Satire in the Morality *Wisdom Who Is Christ*", *Renaissance Papers, 1963*. The Southeastern Renaissance Conference, 41–51.
Boas, Frederick S., *An Introduction to Stuart Drama* (Oxford, The University Press, 1946).
—, *An Introduction to Tudor Drama* (Oxford, The Clarendon Press, 1933).
—, *Shakespeare and His Predecessors* (New York, Charles Scribner's Sons, 1896).
—, *Thomas Heywood* (London, Williams and Northgate, Ltd., 1950).
Bond, R. Warwick (ed.), "On the Relation of These Plays to Latin and Italian Comedy and to the Dutch Education Drama", *Early Plays from the Italian* (Oxford, The Clarendon Press, 1911), xv–cxviii.
Bradbrook, Muriel C., *The Growth and Structure of Elizabethan Comedy* (London, Chatto and Windus, 1955).
—, "Virtue is the True Nobility — A Study of the Structure of *All's Well That Ends Well*", *The Review of English Studies*, I, New Series 4 (October, 1950), 289–301.
Brooke, C. F., Tucker, *The Tudor Drama* (Boston, New York, and Chicago, Houghton Mifflin Company, 1911).
Burton, Ernest James, *The British Theatre: Its Repertory and Practice, 1100–1900* (London, Jenkins, 1960).
Campbell, Oscar J., *Shakespeare's Satire* (London, Oxford University Press, 1943).
Chambers, E. K., *The Elizabethan Stage*, 4 vols. (Oxford, The Clarendon Press, 1923).
—, *The Mediaeval Stage*, 2 vols. (London, Oxford University Press, 1903).
Coghill, Nevill, "The Basis of Shakespearian Comedy", *Essays and Studies, 1950*, Vol. III, New Series (London, John Murray, 1950), 1–28.
Coogan, Sister Mary Philippa, *An Interpretation of the Moral Play, Mankind* (Washington, D. C., The Catholic University Press, 1947).
Courthope, W. J., *A History of English Poetry*, Vol. I (New York, Macmillan and Co., 1895).
Craig, Hardin, *The Enchanted Glass* (New York, Oxford University Press, 1936).
—, *English Religious Drama of the Middle Ages* (Oxford, The Clarendon Press, 1955).
—, "Morality Plays and Elizabethan Drama", *The Shakespeare Quarterly*, I (April, 1950), 64–72.
Craik, T. W., *The Tudor Interlude – Stage, Costume, and Acting* (Leicester, The University Press, 1958).
Creizenach, Wilhelm, "Chapter III, The Early Religious Drama, Miracle Plays and Moralities", *The Cambridge History of English Literature*, edited by A. W. Ward and A. E. Waller, Vol. V, Part I (New York, The Macmillan Company; Cambridge, The University Press, 1933), 40–67.
—, *The English Drama in the Age of Shakespeare*. Translated by Cecile Hugon and revised by Wilhelm Creizenach (Philadelphia and London, J. B. Lippincott Company and Sidgwick and Jackson, Limited, 1916).
Cunningham, Dolora Gallagher, "The Doctrine of Repentance as a Formal

Principle in Some Elizabethan Plays", unpublished Ph. D. dissertation (Stanford University, 1953).
Cushman, L. W., *The Devil and the Vice in the English Dramatic Literature Before Shakespeare* (Halle, Max Niemeyer, 1900).
Dessen, Alan, "The 'Estates' Morality Play", *Studies in Philology*, LXII (January, 1965), 121–136.
Doran, Madeleine, *Endeavors of Art* (Madison, The University of Wisconsin Press, 1963).
Farnham, Willard, *The Medieval Heritage of Elizabethan Tragedy* (New York, Barnes & Noble, Inc., 1936, reprinted with corrections, 1956).
Feldman, A. Bronson, "Dutch Humanism and the Tudor Dramatic Tradition", *Notes and Queries*, 197 (August 16, 1952), 357–360.
Frye, Northrop, *Anatomy of Criticism* (Princeton, Princeton University Press, 1957).
Gayley, Charles Mills (ed.), "An Historical View of the Beginnings of English Comedy", *Representative English Comedies: From the Beginning to Shakespeare*, Vol. I (New York, The Macmillan Company, 1903), xiii–xcii.
Habicht, Werner, "The *Wit*-Interludes and the Form of Pre-Shakespearean 'Romantic Comedy'", *Renaissance Drama*, edited by S. Schoenbaum, Vol. VIII (Evanston, Northwestern University Press, 1965), 73–88.
Harbage, Alfred, *Annals of English Drama, 975–1700*, revised by S. Schoenbaum (London, Metheuen and Co., Ltd., 1964).
Hardison, O. B., Jr., *Christian Rite and Christian Drama in the Middle Ages* (Baltimore, The Johns Hopkins Press, 1965).
Herrick, Marvin, T., *Comic Theory in the Sixteenth Century*, "Illinois Studies in Language and Literature", Vol. XXIV, Nos. 1–2. (Urbana, The University of Illinois Press, 1950).
—, *Tragicomedy*, "Illinois Studies in Language and Literature", No. 39. (Urbana, Illinois Press, 1955).
Hogrefe, Pearl, *The Sir Thomas More Circle* (Urbana, The University of Illinois Press, 1959).
Kinsman, Robert, "Skelton's *Magnyfycence*: The Strategy of The 'Olde Sayde Sawe'", *Studies in Philology*, LXIII (April, 1966), 99–125.
Kolve, V. A., *The Play Called Corpus Christi* (London, Edward Arnold Ltd., 1966).
Knights, L. C., *Drama and Society in the Age of Jonson* (London, Chatto and Windus, 1937).
Lawrence, William Witherle, *Shakespeare's Problem Comedies* (New York, The Macmillan Company, 1931).
Mackenzie, Roy W., *The English Moralities from the Point of View of Allegory* (Boston and London, Ginn and Company, 1914).
Matthews, Brander, "The Medieval Drama", *Modern Philology*, I (June, 1903), 71–94.
Moore, John B., *The Comic and the Realistic in English Drama* (Chicago, The University of Chicago Press, 1925).
Nicoll, Allardyce, *British Drama: An Historical Survey from the Beginnings to the Present Time*, 4th ed. (London, George G. Harrap and Co., Ltd., 1949).

Parrott, Thomas Marc and Ball, Robert Hamilton, *A Short View of Elizabethan Drama* (New York, Charles Scribner's Sons, 1943).
Pettet, E. C., *Shakespeare and the Romance Tradition* (London, Staples Press, 1949).
Pollard, Alfred, W., *English Miracle Plays, Moralities, and Interludes* (Oxford, The Clarendon Press, 1890).
Presson, Robert K., "Marston's *Dutch Courtizan*: The Study of an Attitude in Adaptation", *The Journal of English and Germanic Philology*, LV (July, 1955), 406–13.
Prosser, Eleanor, *Drama and Religion in the English Mystery Plays*, "Stanford Studies in Language and Literature", XXIII. (Stanford, Stanford University Press, 1961).
Ristine, Frank Humphrey, *English Tragicomedy, Its Origin and History* (New York, The Columbia University Press, 1910).
Rossiter, A. P., *Early English Drama* (London, Hutchinson's University Library, 1950).
Ryan, Lawrence V., "Doctrine and Dramatic Structure in *Everyman*", *Speculum* (October, 1957), 722–735.
Schelling, Felix E., *English Drama* (London, J. M. Dent & Sons, Ltd., 1914).
Sensabaugh, George F., "Platonic Love in Shirley's *The Lady of Pleasure*", *A Tribute to George Coffin Taylor*, edited by Arnold Williams (Richmond, Virginia, The University of North Carolina Press by The William Byrd Press, 1952), 168–177.
Snyder, Susan, "The Left Hand of God: Despair in Medieval and Renaissance Tradition", *Studies in the Renaissance*, Vol. XII (New York, The Renaissance Society of America, 1965), 18–59.
Spencer, Theodore, *Shakespeare and the Nature of Man*, 2nd ed. (New York, The Macmillan Company, 1961).
Spivack, Bernard, *Shakespeare and the Allegory of Evil* (New York, Columbia University Press, 1958).
Symonds, John Addington, *Shakespeare's Predecessors in the English Drama*, New ed. (London, Smith, Elder, and Co., 1900).
Ten Brink, Bernhard, *History of English Literature*, translated by William Clarke Robinson, Vol. II (New York, Henry Holt and Co., 1893).
Thorp, Willard, *The Triumph of Realism in Elizabethan Drama, 1558–1612*, "Princeton Studies in English", No. 3. (Princeton, Princeton University Press, 1928).
Tillyard, W. M. W., *The Elizabethan World Picture* (New York, The Macmillan Company, 1944).
—, *Shakespeare's Problem Plays* (London, Chatto and Windus, 1950).
Varma, R. S. "Philosophical and Moral Ideas in *The Marriage of Wit and Science*", *Philological Quarterly*, XLIV (January, 1965), 120–122.
Waith, Eugene M., *The Pattern of Tragicomedy in Beaumont and Fletcher* (New Haven, Yale University Press, 1952).
Wickham, Glynne, *Early English Stages, 1300 to 1600, Volume One, 1300 to 1576* (London, Routledge and Kegan Paul, 1959).
Williams, Arnold, *The Drama of Medieval England* (Michigan State University Press, 1961).

Wright, Louis B., "Social Aspects of Some Belated Moralities", *Anglia* (1930), 107-148.
Wynne, Arnold, *The Growth of English Drama* (Oxford, The Clarendon Press, 1914).
Zesmer, David M., *Guide to English Literature from Beowulf through Chaucer and Medieval Drama.* "College Outline Series", (New York, Barnes & Noble, Inc., 1961).

# INDEX

*Acolastus*, 138, 140–43, 150
action 14, 44, 88–89, 128–29, 132–33; morality actions, 44–48
*Adelphi*, 26
allegory, 41–42, 88, 91, 131–32, 142
*All Fooles*, 24, 26–29, 30
*All's Well That Ends Well*, 13, 16–17, 106–09, 130, 131, 134
*Apology for Actors, An*, 134–35
*As You Like It*, 24–26, 33–34

Beaumont, Francois, 24; tragi-comedy in Beaumont and Fletcher, 34–35; See also *A King and No King*
Bevington, David, 42
bible, 102, 106, 138, 139
Body and Soul, Debate of: see Debate of the Soul and Body
Bradbrook, Muriel, 111

*Castell of Perseverance, The*, 40, 42, 43, 45, 46, 47, 48, 49, 50, 51, 52–53, 54–55, 56, 57, 58, 59, 60, 66, 67, 68, 69, 70
Chambers, E. K., 45, 70, 112
Chapman, George, 13, 24, 26, 99, 101. See also *All Fooles* and *Eastward Ho*
Cinthio, 20
Coghill, Nevill, 25
comedy, 15, 19–20, 24, 38, 90, 133–36. See also *All Fooles, As You Like It, Supposes, Volpone*, Italian comedy, Latin comedy, romantic comedy, and satirical comedy
Coming of Death, The, 45, 47–48
Conflict of Vices and Virtues, The 45–46, 48
*Contention Between Liberality and Prodigality, The*, 81–82
courtesan, 16, 17, 22, 93, 95, 96, 98–99, 125, 129
Craig, Hardin, 15, 42
Creizenach, Wilhelm, 45
Cunningham, Dolora Gallagher, 108

*Damon and Pythias*, 34
Dance of Death, The, 45
Debate of the Heavenly Graces, 45, 47
Debate of the Soul and Body, 45, 46–47
"Defence of Poesie, The", 134
Dekker, Thomas, 13, 98, 102, 109, 119, 125. See also *The Honest Whore, Part I, The Honest Whore, Part II, If This Be Not a Good Play, the Devil Is In It*, and *Match Me in London*
*Disobedient Child, The*, 138, 146–48, 150
*Dutch Curtezan, The*, 13, 16–17, 95–98, 129, 136

## 162 INDEX

*Eastward Ho*, 13, 16—17, 99—101
education drama, 138—150. See also *Misogonus*
Edward, Richard, 34
Elyot, Sir Thomas, 133
*English Traveller, The*, 34
*Everyman*, 40, 42—43, 44, 46, 47, 48, 49, 50, 51, 52, 54, 55, 56, 57, 58, 59, 60, 61, 68, 71

*Faire Maide of Bristow, The*, 13, 16—17, 93—95, 128, 129, 132, 133, 136
*Farewell to Military Profession*, 20
Fletcher, John, 24; tragi-comedy in Beaumont and Fletcher, 34—35. See also *A King and No King*
*Four Elements, The Nature of; The Interlude of*. See *Nature of the Four Elements, The*
Fullonius, 140

Gascoigne, George, 24, 29, 34, 138, 148. See also *The Glasse of Government* and *Supposes*
*Glasse of Government, The*, 34, 138, 148—50
Gnaphaues, 140
Greene, Robert, 13, 102, 104. See also *A Looking Glasse for London and England*

Harbage, Alfred, 15
Harington, Sir John, 133—34
*Heautontimorumenos*, 26
*Hecatommithi*, 20
Heavenly Graces, Debate of the. See Debate of the Heavenly Graces
Heywood, Thomas, 13, 16, 34, 117, 134—35. See also *How a Man May Chuse a Good Wife from a Bad* and *The Wise-Woman of Hogsdon*
*Histrio-Mastix*, 13, 111—13, 129, 130, 131, 132, 134
Hogrefe, Pearl, 68
*Honest Whore, The*, Part I, 13, 16—17, 98—99, 131; Part II, 13, 16—17, 125, 130, 131
*How a Man May Chuse a Good Wife from a Bad*, 16—24, 44, 89, 92, 116; as comedy, 19—20, 38—39; comparison with *All Fooles*, 26—29; comparison with *As You Like It*, 24—26; comparison with a *A King and No King*, 35—38; comparison with *Supposes*, 29—30; comparison with *Volpone*, 30—33; morality elements, 21—23, 38—39, 63—64; novella source, 20—21, 23; printing of editions, 16; relationship with other morality-patterned comedies, 16—17
*Hyckescorner*, 71—72, 89

*If This Be Not a Good Play, the Devil Is In It*, 13, 109—11, 129, 130, 131, 134
*Impatient Poverty*, 79—81, 87
Ingelend, Thomas, 138, 146. See also *The Disobedient Child*
*I Suppositi*, 29
Italian comedy, 24, 38; *Supposes*, example of, 29—30

Johnson, Laurence, 13, 104. See also *Misogonus*
Jonson, Ben, 13, 24, 30—31, 32, 99, 101, 120. See also *Eastward Ho, The Staple of News*, and *Volpone*

*King and No King, A*, 24, 35—38

INDEX 163

*Lady of Pleasure, The*, 13, 122—24, 130, 131
Latin comedy, 26, 29—30, 38, 105, 106, 117, 118—19, 139, 140, 141, 149; *All Fooles*, example of, 26—29
Lindsay, David, 84. See also *Ane Pleasant Satyre of the Thrie Estaitis*
Lodge, Thomas, 13, 102. See also *A Looking Glasse for London and England*
*London Prodigal, The*, 13, 16—17, 115—17, 130, 131, 132—33
*Looking Glasse for London and England, A*, 13, 102—04, 113, 129, 131, 133, 134
*Lusty Juventus*, 73—74, 87—88

Mackenzie, Roy, 41, 45
Macropedius, 140
*Magnyfycence*, 45, 82—84, 85, 89
*Mankind*, 40, 43—44, 46, 49, 50—51, 52, 53, 55, 57, 58, 59, 60, 61, 71, 84
Marston, John, 13, 95, 99, 101, 111. See also *The Dutch Curtezan, Eastward Ho*, and *Histrio-Mastix*
*Match Me in London*, 13, 119—20, 130, 131, 134
Medwall, Henry, 66. See also *Nature*
Middleton, John, 13, 98. See also *The Honest Whore, Part I*
*miles gloriousus*, 38
*Miseries of Enforced Marriage, The*, 13, 125—28, 129, 130, 131, 132, 133, 135
*Misogonus*, 13, 104—06, 130, 133, 138, 143, 150
morality actions, The Conflict of Vices and Virtues, 45—46, 48; The Coming of Death, 45, 47—48; The Dance of Death, 45; The Debate of the Soul and Body, 45, 46—47; The Debate of the Heavenly Graces, 45, 47; The Summons of Death, 45, 48; The Reconciliation of the Heavenly Virtues, 45
morality, elements, formal elements, 14—15, 62—63; allegory, 41—42; character groupings, 60—62; Christian frame, 41; didactic intention, 42—44; spiritual vision, 59—60; structure, 48—59; education drama, relationship to, 138—50; morality-patterned comedies, changes in, 91—92; parody of, 99—101; tudor interludes, changes in, 66, 89—90
morality-patterned comedy, as comedy 133—36; comparison with moral interludes, 91—92, 128—33; comparison with the morality play, 91—92, 129—33; core plays, 16—17, 17—24, 92—101; definition, 14, 63—64; formal elements, 128—33
*Mundus et Infans*, 68—70, 89

*Nature*, 66—68, 70
*Nature of the Four Elements, The*, 74—76, 88, 89
New comedy. See Latin comedy
*Nice Wanton, A Preaty Interlude Called*, 138, 143—46, 150

Palsgrave, John, 138, 140, 143. See also *Acolastus*
pastoral romance, 24
patient wife, testing of, 119, 120, 125
*Pleasant Satyre of the Thrie Estaitis, Ane*, 84—85
plot, 14, 44, 88—89, 91, 128—29
political plays. See State, welfare of
*Pride of Life*, 40, 84
prodigal, 16, 80, 81—82, 99—101, 115—18, 120—22, 125, 126—27, 128—29, 130, 131, 132, 141, 146, 147

prodigality and liberality, contention over, 79—82, 81—82, 121—22
prodigal son, parable of, 106, 138, 139—40, 141, 143

Ramsey, Robert Lee, 44—45, 51
Rastell, John, 74. See also *The Nature of the Four Elements*
realism, tendency toward, 68, 72, 88—89, 132—33
*Rebelles*, 140
Reconciliation of the Heavenly Virtues, The, 45
Redford, John, 74. See also *The Play of Wyt and Science*
religious controversy, 73—74, 87—88
*Respublica*, 85—86
Richards, Thomas, 13, 104. See also *Misogonus*
Rich, Barnaby, 20
Ristine, Frank, 35
romantic comedy, 24, 38; *As You Like It*, example of, 24—26
Rudd, Anthony, 13, 104. See also *Misogonus*
Ryan, Lawrence, 60

*sacre rappresentazioni*, 139
satirical comedy, 24, 29, 38, 122; *Volpone*, example of, 30—33
Sensabaugh, George, 122
Schelling, Felix, 41
Shakespeare, William, 13, 24, 106. See also *All's Well That Ends Well* and *As You Like It*
Shirley, James, 13, 122. See also *The Lady of Pleasure*
Sidney, Sir Phillip, 134
Skelton, John, 82. See also *Magnyfycence*
social criticism, 53, 81, 125, 127—28, 132
spiritual vision, 15, 39, 56—57, 59—60, 62—63, 130
Spivack, Bernard, 45
*Staple of News, The*, 13, 120—22, 129, 131, 133, 135
State, welfare of, 82—86, 87, 102—04, 109—11, 112—15, 129, 131
structure, 14, 38—39, 41, 44, 48—59, 62—63, 66, 89, 91, 129—30
Summons of Death, The, 45, 48
*Supposes*, 24, 29—30

Terence, 26, 139, 140, 149
Thorp, Willard, 15
tragi-comedy, 33—35; *A King and No King*, example of, 35—38
tudor interludes, 65—90; action, 88—89; differences from morality plays, 66, 89—90; freshness of details, 68; plot, 88—89; structure, 89; types: scope of Mankind's earthly life, 66—70; religious controversy, 73—74; education, 74—78; rightful prosperity, 79—82; welfare of state, 82—86

Volder, Wilhelm de, 140, 142
*Volpone*, 24, 30—33

Waith, Eugene, 35, 37
*Wealth and Health, An Interlude of*, 86
Wever, R., 73. See also *Lusty Juventus*
Wilkins, George, 13, 125. See also *The Miseries of Enforced Marriage*
*Wisdom*, 40, 43, 46, 49, 50, 51—52, 53, 55, 56, 57, 58, 59, 61, 71
*Wise-Woman of Hogsdon, The*, 13, 16—17, 117—19, 130, 131, 136

Wright, Louis, B., 53, 81
*Wyt and Science, The Play of,* 76—78, 88—89, 129

*Youth,* 72—73

Zesmer, David M., 41—42

3215

OHIO UNIVERS